THE LITTLE RED BOX OF MANAGEMENT TOOLS

THE LITTLE RED BOX OF MANAGEMENT TOOLS

HOW CONSERVATIVE MANAGEMENT PRACTICES COULD HAVE HELPED US AVOID THE MESS WE'RE IN

JIM OLSON

Tate Publishing & *Enterprises*

The Little Red Box of Management Tools

Published by Tate Publishing & Enterprises, LLC
127 E. Trade Center Terrace | Mustang, Oklahoma 73064 USA
1.888.361.9473 | www.tatepublishing.com

Tate Publishing is committed to excellence in the publishing industry. The company reflects the philosophy established by the founders, based on Psalm 68:11,
"The Lord gave the word and great was the company of those who published it."

Cover design by Jeff Fisher
Interior design by Stephanie Woloszyn

Published in the United States of America

ISBN: 978-1-61663-840-5
1. Business & Economics / Leadership 2. Business & Economics / Management
10.08.04

ACKNOWLEDGMENTS

THANKS TO MY WIFE FOR INCENTIVE;
MY STUDENTS FOR CURIOSITY;
DEAN ROGER WEIKLE FOR OPPORTUNITY
AND DR. KEITH BENSON FOR FEEDBACK
AND ENCOURAGEMENT.

A WALK WITH THE WALRUS

(APOLOGIES TO LEWIS CARROLL)

"The time has come," the Walrus said,
"to talk of many things."

"Of commoditization, customization, and globalization
Of the useful insights diversity brings
Of aspiration, inspiration, and preparation
Of methods, meaning, and morality
Of evolution, revolution, and competition
Of tools, teamwork, and integrity
Of looking, learning, and avoiding rot
Of why the Brit lost to the Hottentot*
And of curiosity, creativity,
and continuous improvement."

*More apologies for calling
Zulus Hottentots in order to forge a rhyme.

TABLE OF CONTENTS

If you acquired this book to help you catch up on the latest trends in management theory, please take it back. It does not offer or examine new business insights. Instead, it is a short, simple, sensible and—I hope—useful collection of conservative management concepts and practices based on lectures I use to teach college business school students. My audiences are full of hormones, hope, and impatience, which combine to produce a short attention span. Consequently, the book takes an approach favored by Mark Twain, who said, "If I'd had more time, I would have written a shorter book." [1]

My primary purpose is to simplify and clarify proven management concepts so that young people can grasp, remember, and use them. Think of this *slim* book as the Cliff's Notes for the *stout* seven-hundred-page texts used in many college-level management courses. I believe students need both slim and stout to learn efficiently and effectively. I also admit to a secondary purpose. The current economic mess and the state of the company where I learned and developed most of my management skills have sparked some thoughts I need to get off my chest.

I acquired most of my business knowledge during thirty-five years in the auto industry, where I observed good and bad management at close range. Now I'm trying to pass along some of my observations during a post-retirement teaching career. This dual-purpose book is part of my effort. It contains concepts from textbooks as well as business and history books and magazines in the ever-changing stack next to my reading chair at home. It also describes real-world experiences, some of my opinions about current business developments, and thoughts triggered by student questions and discussions with colleagues.

I believe that the primary asset I bring to teaching is a compulsion to tell stories drawn from my experience in an effort to make management techniques as clear and memorable as I can. The effort is forced upon me by audiences harder to engage than the board of directors and Congressional committees I frequently faced. Furthermore, the members of the audience change every three months, requiring a continuous treasure hunt for new ways to energize myself and engage them.

My search for new ways led to a "toolbox" approach in which I give my students a set of management tools and techniques they can reach for when facing problems and opportunities. I also urge them to patiently think things through with a practical, fact-focused approach. In their end-of-semester instructor evaluations, many have said this works for them.

This project is my wife's fault. Like me, her father ended his business career without specific post-retirement plans. Deprived of adrenalin and facing boredom, he promptly fretted himself into a minor heart attack—a parental lesson that his daughter has never forgotten.

Consequently, when I retired, she said, "Go find something useful to do, *now!*" I took her advice and contacted the local university. The result is my position as an executive in residence and adjunct instructor at Winthrop University's College of Business Administration in Rock Hill, South Carolina—an opportunity for which I am grateful.

My college days never hinted that I'd end up teaching at one. In 1964, I graduated with a BA in English literature from Stanford University, where I earned B's and C's while surreptitiously majoring in girls. Then—courtesy of the US Navy—I spent several years in Vietnam and San Francisco, where I learned my first management lessons and began to grow up. A GI bill master's degree in journalism at Northwestern University led to a job in the Public Affairs Division at Ford Motor Company, where, over 16 years, I rose to mid-level management.

THE TOYOTA WAY

Then, in 1985, Toyota called. The Japanese juggernaut, as it later became known, was about to begin a rapid expansion in North America. Worried about potential public and political backlash, Toyota wanted an experienced American to form an external affairs division (government relations; public relations; product publicity; philanthropy; corporate social responsibility; and, later, shareholder relations and corporate advertising). The assignment was to identify and work with stakeholders to build public and political acceptance for Toyota's growth in North America. Oversight of the company's small-but-growing US motorsports program was thrown in as an additional inducement to leave gray Detroit for sunny Los Angeles.

It was an exciting opportunity to participate in the rapid growth of a company already becoming known for its successful and far-sighted management practices. Both my wife and mother-in-law, who lived with us at the time, agreed. So I took the job and my real education began.

Toyota is unique. The precepts that define its policies and practices were first stated at its founding more than seventy years ago. Although the words have evolved, the substance has changed very little. At its core, the "Toyota way" always has been based on customer satisfaction, respect for people, continuous improvement, hatred of waste, and love of challenge. I learned that Toyota people are expected to:

- Be humble and courteous
- Hate waste, revere efficiency, and create value
- Recognize customers as the company's most important stakeholders
- Respect the individual, but use the creative and collaborative power of teamwork
- Realize that perfection is *never* possible, but improvement *always* is
- Go and see because true understanding requires firsthand experience rather than secondhand reports
- Seek opportunities and challenge competitors

- Embrace the responsibilities of citizenship wherever the company does business
- And, finally, always maintain a margin of safety and prepare for a potential downside

The "learning" corporate culture these principles forged is ethical, disciplined, conservative, focused on excellence, constant at its core, adaptive at its margin, and hyper competitive. Unfortunately, I believe the primary causes of Toyota's recent stumbles also lurk in the company's otherwise admirable core.

I arrived at Toyota as the company reached a historic turning point. Although it was Japan's biggest and the world's fifth-largest automaker, Toyota still was largely a national company, serving most of its overseas markets with products made in Japan. But the massive build-up that would make it the world's biggest automaker and a very large presence in many overseas markets was beginning. As a cultural and political facilitator in what would become Toyota's biggest market, I was ideally placed to observe some of the methods that make the company such a powerful competitor.

THE MORE THINGS CHANGE, THE MORE THEY STAY THE SAME

I've read articles hailing the arrival of "virtual" companies that find and coordinate free-standing capabilities to create a product or service—similar to renting chunks of "cloud" analysis time from a computer center somewhere in the world instead of creating in-house capability. But, as we'll see, whether you are the CEO of a traditional company with a recognizable organization chart and full-time employees or head of a virtual enterprise that directly owns nothing, most of the principles defining what you do, why you do it, and how you go about it are the same and the tools and techniques similar. Your goal is to create a useful and attractive product or service and then make money by finding and delighting buyers in ways that will form lasting relationships competitors can't breach. That's why the tools described in this book apply to all businesses—large and small, bricks or clicks.

At Toyota, I learned that in order to succeed these sensible tools must be based on ethics and integrity that build stakeholder trust and support. They also stress the collaborative creation of genuine value; evolve slowly; require long-term, disciplined application; and are embedded in a company's corporate culture. At the best companies, the culture is the "leader" and management's primary task is to preserve it, keep it relevant to the competitive situation and assure that everyone in the company understands and abides by it. Companies are primarily people, processes and culture. *The third tells the first how to do the second.* If the culture is not both eternal and adaptive, success will be fleeting because the company's sense of self won't last and its business model won't stay in step with the changing environment. This task is the responsibility of the company's managers, and the best of them realize that they are teachers as well as businesspeople.

Strengthening and evolving the culture has become even more important in today's flatter, more horizontal organizations. As power is decentralized and leadership distributed, culture and training must provide the compass, guiding the individual daily decisions and actions that create the company's reputation and lead to long-term success.

For example, as Toyota rapidly expanded its global operations and hired more than 100,000 new employees over a decade, the top managers in Japan tried to assure that all members of the company clear around the world fully understood and practiced the "Toyota way"—a difficult task at which I believe they have been only partially successful.

I also learned that effective management tools form an interlinked system that must be applied in a balanced way and as a whole to be fully successful. A couple of pirated techniques planted in an inefficient and ineffective corporate culture cannot provide a foundation for lasting success. Firms trying to quickly copy the Toyota production system (TPS) without fully comprehending its deep organizational roots soon learned this lesson.

The conservatism emphasized in this little book is timely because it is being written as the global economy is experiencing a nearly unprecedented financial meltdown with potentially far-reaching consequences. I believe that much of this situation is the result of personal greed, dysfunctional corporate cultures, and reckless disregard for the conservative business principles I and others like me are trying to teach the next generation of Main Street and Wall Street managers.

Business Week described the path to perdition this way. "The smartest people were telling us that Wall Street had vanquished the business cycle by gaining mastery over risk. No mortgage was too absurd, no leverage too great, no structured product too reckless when risk-spreading models were so brilliantly engineered. Common sense laws no longer applied. And then the bubble burst."[2]

Any book about management, including this one, skates across the surface. You can familiarize students with the principles underlying ethical, efficient, and effective management; illustrate them with stories from your experience; and explain how events like the current meltdown might have been avoided or minimized. But no amount of lecturing, examples, and simulations can teach tomorrow's managers how to effectively wield the tools. That requires on-the-job experience such as helping your company work its way through a credit meltdown. Only fingers burned and lessons learned can drive the techniques home and teach managers how to balance principle with pragmatism and discipline with creativity. Because it is mostly common sense, basic management is relatively easy to comprehend. But it is difficult to do.

Although I learned other management concepts from the US Navy and Ford Motor Company, those I acquired during my nineteen years at Toyota have most profoundly affected my outlook and comprise much of what I now teach. But before we get to that, let me introduce and thank my teaching coach.

YODA

Before turning me loose with paying customers, the business school dean wanted to be sure I knew something about teaching. So he assigned me a coach. For a semester, I co-taught management with Dr. Keith Benson, a short powerhouse adept at infecting students with high standards, curiosity, ethics and enthusiasm. Think of him as Yoda.

The first technique he taught me was, "If you're not enthusiastic, they won't be. So stay on your feet and *move!*" It's amazing how many speakers ignore this energetic "tent-preacher" technique. His second suggestion was, "Watch their eyes. When they glaze over, pitch the power point and do something to wake them up."

I learned many other things sitting on a stool in the corner of a classroom watching Keith prowl and prod. Because he and I wanted to learn from one another, our team approach created collaboration (Benson=principle; Olson=example) beneficial to our students. I called us Heckle and Jeckle, and we had fun. What a great lesson: combine teaching with fun. And although we have not team taught again, the input and feedback I continue to receive from Keith helped me tackle this project.

OF BICYCLES AND BUSINESS

I think of good management as the bicycle you had when you were young. If your parents were generous or you reaped a lot of paper-route, weeding, and lawn-mowing revenue, you might have owned one of those lightweight bikes with re-curved handlebars, skinny tires, and little levers that enabled you to change gear as you pedaled along. You'd flip a lever and downshift so that each pedal stroke would take more effort but also propel you further and faster. Together, frame, transmission, wheels, and rider formed an integrated system designed to maintain balance, adapt to the terrain, and reach goals efficiently and effectively.

In most new models, the manufacturer would re-engineer the gears, lighten the frame, or improve the tires to gain more speed with less effort. That's exactly what good management does: continuously adapt and improve a company's workforce, processes, structure, and technology to decrease what goes in and increase what comes out. Add direction and destination to this pursuit of efficiency, and you have the essence of sound management theory.

The persistently urgent heart of this approach is a process called "Plan, Do, Check, Act (PDCA)." If applied properly, it yields the continuous improvement Japanese businesspeople call *kaizen.* The technique has been around for decades under this name and in other forms such as Six Sigma. Some of these forms go way back. For example, one of the most successful coaches ever, John Wooden, used a form of PDCA to go forty years without a losing season and lead the UCLA basketball team to seven consecutive national titles. He first wrote down his personal "continuous improvement" methods in 1934, three years before Toyota Motor Corporation (which has helped to popularize PDCA) was founded. Winning was not Wooden's primary goal. Instead, he found the best players he could and focused all his effort on assuring that each of them played to his full potential. Winning was a byproduct of this individual self-improvement. [3]

MANAGEMENT DEFINED

> In his 1917 book *Industrial Management,* French expert Henri Fayol defined management as "planning, organizing, leading and controlling money, manpower, material and Information to achieve organizational goals efficiently and effectively."
>
> (These are Fayol's concepts, but my words)

Fayol's definition dictates this book's format and title. Imagine you are standing in front of a red, steel toolbox with wheels. Its four half-open drawers are empty but labeled. The top drawer says, "Planning." The second is, "Organizing." The third is, "Leading." And at the bottom is, "Controlling." Because it has wheels, you can tow the toolbox along on your business journey. But first you have to fill it with tools. Let's begin with ...

The most successful football coach ever, Notre Dame's Knute Rockne, said, "The secret of genius is an infinite capacity for taking pains." [1] There are few better examples of this insight than the 1879 battle of Islandlwana in what is now South Africa. It pitted approximately four thousand highly trained British troops armed with expertise, arrogance, and Martini-Henry rifles against twenty-two thousand wily Zulus armed with courage, spears, and cowhide shields. Because of their firepower and previous successes, the British expected to win the battle despite the more than five to one numerical advantage enjoyed by the Zulus. [2]

However, due to overconfidence and under-preparation, the British were outmaneuvered. In addition, their ammunition was packed in tin-lined, steel-strapped cases requiring a special tool to open. Oops! Someone misplaced most of the tools. Unable to get enough ammunition quickly enough, the British were overwhelmed; and most were slaughtered. Let's hope the officers who made invalid assumptions and took insufficient pains were among the casualties.

What's the primary lesson for business? *It's always management's fault.*

Rockne's observation and the battle of Islandlwana clearly contain other business applications as well:

- Never underestimate a competitor.
- Always overdo your preparations.
- Pay close attention to the terrain.

These lessons are the heart of good belt-and-suspenders corporate planning, which I think of as *what keeps you on your feet when life pulls the rug out from under them.* Good managers, particularly those who have climbed well up the corporate ladder, have learned to be conscientious, conservative, skeptical, and sure-footed. In fact, conservatism and "taking pains" are primary hallmarks of the planning process underlying good management at successful corporations. Let's look at how many of them go about it.

The ideal planning process starts with a corporate-wide communication loop designed to harvest expertise, forge shared understanding, create organizational alignment, and build employee ownership of and commitment to the plan it produces.

Like many other corporate processes, planning begins at the top and flows downhill. But then, if done properly, it defies gravity and flows back uphill. This is because a successful communication loop always ends where it began: 1) sender encodes and sends message, 2) receiver decodes message and sends feedback conveying understanding or seeking clarification, 3) sender and receiver repeat this loop until shared understanding is achieved.

This communication process takes place inside a particular corporate culture created by core ideology ("Who are we?") and core purpose ("What are we here to do?"). The answers to these questions form the company's DNA, which determines its corporate culture. Like a star on the horizon, this DNA evolves very slowly, if at all. It sets the company's direction by telling everyone inside how to make and take the hundreds of daily decisions and actions that define the company, create its reputation, and build (or destroy) its brand strength. It is a big, self-centering gyroscope that you hope is exactly mimicked by a little gyroscope inside each employee. Together, big and little keep the company balanced and on course.

Core ideology need not be spelled out. For example, when you visit the corporate campus of athletic equipment manufacturer Nike, there is no big, blinking sign saying "Core Ideology." Instead, the photos of winning athletes all over the place graphically hint that the company culture is something like, "We live to support the thrill of victory."

A clear and passionate ideological statement can be useful in recruiting the best and brightest. As management expert Peter Drucker said, "Because they can work anywhere, the best people are volunteers."[3] This also supports my conclusion that effective core ideology is aimed primarily *in,* not *out.* Its chief purpose is to inspire, motivate, and focus employees, not to differentiate the company from competitors—although it often does both.

Successful companies with strong and ethical core ideologies tend to have a *stakeholder,* rather than a *shareholder,* philosophy that includes some commitment to make a useful contribution to society.

Although maximizing shareholder wealth is important, employees will not sacrifice their hearts, souls, and free time to add a dollar per share to the bottom line. But research has demonstrated that many of them will commit all three if they believe they are creating value for themselves and society as well as the company. Later in this book, I explore some other effects of a stakeholder versus shareholder approach to business.

The planning process begins with a leader's "vision." Imagine that you are the leader. To find your vision, you ask and answer four questions that are the foundation for all effective business planning:

- *What* is our product or service?
- *Who* will buy it?
- *What* do they want in the product, sales and service experiences?
- *How* can we give it to them in ways that will energize us, separate us from competitors, capture customer loyalty, make money and build sustainable competitive advantage?

Values ("What do we hold most dear?"), *vision* ("Where are we going?") and *strategy* ("How do we plan to get there?") result from answering these basic questions in detail. Eventually, the information and analysis gathered to fully answer the questions are assembled into the company's business plan.

Once this groundwork is complete, a mission statement ("Why are we here?") is generated to capture corporate purpose, provide direction, and ignite commitment. If it's expressed well and communicated persuasively, this lightning in a bottle can help to motivate and focus employee performance. Unfortunately, many mission statements are "group think" products that try to say too much, spreading employee focus across too many unclear goals. Here are some examples.

CISCO

Cisco solutions provide competitive advantage to our customers through more efficient and timely exchange of information, which in turn leads to cost savings, process efficiencies, and closer relationships with customers, prospects, business partners, suppliers, and employees. [4]

I'll bet this statement was constructed by a room full of bright people during a professionally facilitated off-site planning meeting followed by golf, tennis, drinking, dinner, guest speaker, and more drinking.

Translation: Cisco is the people network. We build *our* customers' competitive edge by enabling them to more efficiently and effectively share information with *their* customers, employees, and business partners.

This version is more economical, if not very inspiring. The first sentence is lifted from Cisco's advertising. What's the lesson? If the advertising agency defines corporate purpose better than the planning department, go with the flow.

AT&T

We are dedicated to being the world's best at bringing people together—giving them easy access to each other and to the information and services they want and need—anytime, anywhere. [5]

Translation: We are the best at bringing people together by giving them access to the information and help they need.

WALMART

We work for you. We think of ourselves as buyers for our customers, and we apply our considerable strengths to get the best value for you. We've built Walmart by acting on behalf of our customers, and that concept continues to propel us. We're working hard to make our customers' shopping easy. [6]

Translation: We help our customers live better by offering top value at low prices every day.

TOYOTA'S NORTH AMERICAN OPERATIONS

We will become America's most *respected* and *accepted* automaker.

I hope the context I have provided makes translation unnecessary.

A good mission statement should "reach" toward bold goals: capturing and communicating corporate purpose in order to fuel and focus employee action.

It won't do so unless it is short; simple; sincere; and, if possible, inspiring.

CLOSING THE LOOP

By hammering out values, vision, mission, and strategy (VVMS), you and your executive team have defined purpose and path. But you still don't have a plan. To get one, you must establish specific goals: determine, assign and allocate the three R's (responsibility, resources, and required results); define timetables; and amplify strategy with detailed tactics. For that, you need help from the people who will carry out the plan.

In the past, Harvard University's insightful Michael Porter maintained that you had to choose either a *differentiation* or a *low-cost* strategy. [7] Either you spend money to differentiate your product by adding features for which you then have to charge a premium or you drive down costs so you can under-price competitors. He maintained that trying to do both (i.e., straddling) would fail to focus and leave the company "caught in the middle."

However, companies such as Toyota have successfully implemented a hybrid strategy, pursuing a low-cost/ high-quality approach with some of their product lines (Toyota and Scion), and using the profits to infuse technology and differentiation into other higher-priced products (Lexus and hybrids). In short, they exert discrete and different focus within divisions. However, Porter is absolutely correct in saying that trying to do both with the same product would likely be confusing and unsuccessful.

Whatever strategy you choose, you need help to flesh out your plan. To get it, you must complete the communication loop that will involve the rest of the organization. So you communicate the VVMS to everyone in the company and ask them to answer three questions in as much detail as they can: 1) How would you improve these ideas? 2) What specific goals would you establish overall and in your area of responsibility? 3) What resources (budget, people, time, etc.) would you need to achieve them?

To answer these questions, the organization usually employs basic planning techniques such as SWOT analysis (strength, weakness, opportunity, threat):

(1) What are our organizational strengths?

(2) What are our organizational weaknesses?

(3) What current opportunities in the outside environment can we take advantage of?

(4) What current threats in the outside environment do we need to defend against?

The information generated by SWOT and other processes provides specific goals; criteria for measuring success (Key Performance Indicators, KPIs; more about this later); resource requests; timetables; suggested roles; and, in some cases, suggested structure. All of this is fed back upstream to top management to close the communication loop. Management then finalizes the plan and directs the organization to implement it.

This planning loop harvests suggested improvements from the organization's collective brain, begins the process of unifying everyone behind the plan and making them feel they own it, and starts to generate the necessary excitement to achieve goals.

CORPORATE SOCIAL RESPONSIBILITY AND THE TRIPLE BOTTOM LINE

Public demands that business work to improve society as well as make a profit stem from America's protestant roots. Over the past thirty years or so, this demand has acquired even more insistance and a formal name. Corporate social responsibility (CSR) requires a company to maximize its positive and minimize its negative impact on society. Like all other business factors, a CSR strategy must be thoroughly defined and included in the company's plan. Today, many companies react to society's continuously growing CSR expectations by reporting results to a triple bottom line—profit, people, planet—at the end of each fiscal year. Note that the first CSR *p* is profit, without which a company cannot survive to fulfill the other two. As Drucker noted, "To do good, you must first do well." [8]

I helped set up Toyota's US philanthropy programs and oversaw them for many years. Most of our investments supported education, particularly if a program had a twist that also would help strengthen the company's environmental reputation.

We benchmarked other large companies to assure that Toyota was among the leaders with a similar focus. We also issued a report annually describing our CSR programs and progress. And finally, we used public opinion research to carefully monitor the growth of CSR expectations and periodically react with new programs to increase our philanthropy and further reduce the environmental impact of our US facilities and products. This "monitor-and-move" strategy is standard operating procedure at many observant companies.

BENCHMARKING, CONVERGING, AND COMMODITIZING

I have ignored a nice-to-have step that many companies employ. Let me correct my oversight by briefly describing benchmarking. It has become fairly standard practice for companies to visit and examine other companies—both inside and outside their industry or market segment—to see if they can pick up ideas for improving their own operations. Even Toyota, an acknowledged leader in manufacturing methods, uses benchmarking from time to time.

Michael Porter has observed an unfortunate side effect of benchmarking he calls "competitive convergence."[9] As competitors more frequently and intensely study and copy one another's methods, their approaches and techniques tend to become similar, which can lead to equality that erodes product uniqueness, undercutting brand strength and customer loyalty. This denies companies the ability to charge a premium that can be invested in improvement.

As competing companies pursue productivity and market share in the same segments, combined production capacity can outrun demand (you usually think the other companies' plants, not yours, are the excess capacity) and their products can become "commoditized," interchangeable with one another in customers' minds.

Customers love this because it puts them in charge, enabling them to demand higher content and quality at a lower price. But it can slowly bankrupt companies. Witness what has happened in the North American steel, airline, and auto industries where market and economic pressure have forced downsizing, merger, and bankruptcy.

PLANS EMERGE, BRACKETING

At this point, the process has produced a plan—or, more precisely, three plans: best-case, likely, and worst-case. Prudent companies usually "bracket" by at least partially constructing the bookend plans on either side of the most likely scenario in an attempt to capture all possible "futures." Later, I'll describe the "what-if" game that drives the bracketing process.

Typically, a company implements the likely case while putting the best- and worst-case scenarios on the shelf in case they are needed. Some go even further by constructing "crisis management" plans for specific potential scenarios. As the scientist Louis Pasteur said, "Chance favors only the prepared mind." [10]

ONE PLANT TOO MANY: TOYOTA OVER-REACHES?

Most conservative companies rarely execute their best-case plan because it can cause them to over-reach and become vulnerable to sudden, unexpected changes in circumstances. I believe Toyota violated this conservative safeguard by switching its primary focus from *better* to *bigger* and building too many plants in too many countries too fast.

Here in North America, I think the tipping point was the decision to enter the full-sized truck market and construct a billion-dollar plant in Texas to fuel the effort. The plant has frequently been idle or underutilized because gas prices rose, the economy shrank and truck sales sank. Underutilized production assets, adverse economic conditions, and the yen's strong exchange rate were the primary factors that caused Toyota to lose money for the first time in 57 years.

Unfortunately, I was part of the American management team that helped convince the Toyota Motor Corporation (TMC) board to build the truck plant. When you become an officer of a TMC subsidiary, you are no longer just in charge of several departments. You join a group of officers charged with running the entire subsidiary. This requires a different mindset and a broader approach–*a responsibility I mostly ignored.* Instead, I allowed an old Washington saying to shape my thinking: "If you're not at the table, you're on the menu." I viewed the Texas plant from the 50-foot perspective of the guy in charge of government relations. To me, it represented more American employees and a big economic contribution in a politically important state, all of which could increase Toyota's political influence and help to secure the company a place at the table.

Instead, I should have taken a 5,000-foot officer's perspective and posed the "what-if" questions responsible top managers at successful companies should ask. This can require you to oppose a majority viewpoint and urge your colleagues to consider risks they don't want to acknowledge. Overcoming the natural human herd instinct to go-along-to-get-along can be difficult.

I also believe TMC was receptive to the truck-plant proposal because an attitude change was underway at our parent company. Within the constant core I admire, there also lurks a "dark side"–confidence that can bloom into arrogant over-reach when fertilized by success and praise. I have learned that pride has two close neighbors—one good and one bad. On its right is competitive spirit, which can generate enthusiasm that improves organizational performance. But on its left is hubris that seduces management to look in the mirror instead of out the window.

Certain of its capabilities and lured by the prospect of becoming global number one, Toyota overreached—outrunning its supply of experienced human resources and expanding its global workforce by more than 100,000 new employees over a decade. This rendered the company incapable of achieving swift growth while also cutting costs and protecting the high product quality that has long been the heart of its brand reputation.

When quality problems began to crop up, I suspect the chief engineers of the offending models were reluctant to take the problems to top management because they would "lose face" by doing so. The result was a record number of reputation-shredding product recalls—nearly nine million vehicles worldwide over an eight-month period—and the biggest fine ($16.4 million) ever levied against an automaker by the National Highway Traffic Safety Administration (NHTSA).

Recalls by all automakers are likely to grow in size and frequency for two reasons: 1) The world's automakers share a stressed and shrinking supplier base 2) Most of them also employ nearly continuous cost-cutting, which (among other things) sharply increases the components shared among their vehicles, driving up the numbers covered by each recall. Although cost savings generated by the gains in economy of scale help their bottom lines, these tactics also make them more vulnerable to widespread quality failures that can undermine public trust in their products.

At the root of Toyota's current situation lie governance failure and internal distrust that hampers decision-making. To stop its bleeding, Toyota needs to slow its rate of growth, rekindle its leadership in product quality, and strongly consider changing its structure to improve reaction speed—particularly in crisis situations. This will require the company to re-balance cost-cutting and product quality with renewed attention to the latter. In a marketplace where customers increasingly experience little difference in the traditional Things Gone Wrong (TGW) quality of a Ford, a Toyota or a Hyundai, Toyota also may need to improve and emphasize effective TGR (Things Gone Right) differentiators such as style, technology and vehicle dynamics.

The company also needs to dig out the internal distrust and flawed communication at the root of its current crisis. Basically, the company did not sufficiently change its mindset, structure and governance processes as it grew from a national company serving overseas markets with Japan-built products into a company with large manufacturing operations all over the world. Instead of sufficiently training and fully empowering the non-Japanese managers of its growing over-seas subsidiaries, the company continued to make most of the important decisions affecting major markets in Japan and then directed regional management to implement them.

This "divide-and-conquer" structure separates decision-making from execution, slowing the company down by hampering communication, planning and cross-training among the company's regional operations that could benefit Toyota. It also sends an unfortunate message to many of Toyota's non-Japanese managers: "We don't fully trust you."

Finally, there is a disagreement on basic strategy within Toyota. The company's founding precepts have always stressed a stakeholder philosophy with the customer at the head of the line. Much of the top management still holds this viewpoint. But concurrent with its strategic shift to bigger rather than better, another contingent of top executives supported a shareholder philosophy. Toyota does not have enough resources to battle itself as well as its competitors. Abraham Lincoln's observation "A house divided against itself cannot stand" during the U.S. civil war applies to Toyota's current situation. Toyota must heal its strategic division and select one pathway out of the wilderness.

Because of its tenacity and capability, I believe Toyota will find ways to rebuild its tattered reputation. But some of the current actions to deal with the market's loss of confidence in the company could have long-term negative effects. For example, Toyota is using substantial consumer purchase incentives to spur sales. This unavoidable tactic could further erode Toyota's strong reputation, which always has enabled it to sell the *product* rather than the *deal.*

In order to retrieve its brand strength and regain momentum, the root causes must be dealt with or the hubris, lack of trust and internal division that led Toyota down the wrong path will block necessary improvements. Meanwhile, the company will learn that leading the parade allows everyone following you to take a clear shot at the target pinned to your backside.

THE TORTOISE AND THE HARE

VVMS, SWOT, benchmarking, bracketing, and what-if comprise the basic process that leads to a final and fully resourced corporate plan. But *change is the only constant,* so you're not done yet. In fact, planning is an endless process requiring continuous observation and adjustment. A competitor launches a new and disruptive technology (example: Record→CD→ MP3) that partially or completely obsoletes your product. A key supplier goes out of business. Your core customers age, forcing you to modify your product to meet their changing capabilities. The birthrate spikes, delivering another "pig-in-a-python" generation to work its way through the market, surprising you with new tastes, challenges, and opportunities. A trade agreement opens new markets overseas. The economy dips into recession. Raw material prices accelerate. Your cost of capital increases as interest rates rise or your credit rating falls. You get hammered by a sudden, major shift in an exchange rate.

These ever-changing factors and many more force planners to continually re-assess the environment and the basic assumptions supporting the company's business model. Based on the results of this perpetual paranoia, management adjusts the bicycle to the new terrain and the plan is re-implemented for another trip. The key consideration is to be observant, open to new ideas and to *always run scared.*

You can't always solve tomorrow's problems with yesterday's solutions. Instead, you must destroy what is no longer valid and invest the savings in creating tomorrow. Companies that forget this get big, slow and saddled with overblown structure. And frequently they end up as corporate road kill.

For example, consider the thirty companies that currently comprise the Dow Jones Industrial Average. Started in 1889 by the editors of *The Wall Street Journal*, the Dow's purpose was to capture a representative mix of US companies that could be used to track the general health of American business. Only four of the thirty companies that constituted the Dow in 1929 remain part of the index today (AT&T, DuPont, GE, and Proctor & Gamble). GM was recently replaced by Cisco. [11] The rest have changed their name, been bought by some other firm, or gone out of business. As noted business book author Jim Collins puts it, "They have fallen from great to good to gone." [12]

Most companies go through the reassessment exercise that keeps them alive, on track, and relevant at least once a year when annual results become available and the budget and plan for the coming fiscal year are constructed. In volatile markets and industries, the process can be virtually continuous. As I noted earlier, it is called plan do check act (PDCA). You plan and then execute the plan, check the results against your goals, improve the plan, and begin again. If you're successful, this never-ending cycle generates continuous improvement—a powerful "tortoise" that can steadily inch competitors to death.

This classic planning process is logical, conservative, and risk-averse. If carried out in a disciplined fashion, it might eventually reach the ultimate goal of all corporations: sustainable competitive advantage. However, in order to attain the goal, it's likely that occasionally, you will have to add a leaping "hare" to the race: a big hairy audacious goal (BHAG). Think of the tortoise as discipline and the hare as creativity. Successful companies learn to balance the two forces, using more of one or the other in order to react to changes in the environment.

A BHAG is a long-term (ten-to-fifteen-year) goal that requires an organization to build new, stronger capabilities. Often, the goal is the implementation of a disruptive new technology that will give the company first-mover advantage. BHAG's usually come from someone in top management who is truly visionary rather than just strategic. BHAG's force companies to gulp for air and run faster. Here are a few examples.

> I will build a motor car for the great multitude … It will be priced so low that any man making a good salary will be able to afford it … When I'm through, everybody will have one, the horse will have disappeared from our highways, the automobile will be taken for granted, and a large number of men will be employed at good wages.
>
> Henry Ford when he founded Ford Motor Company [4]

> I want twice the fuel economy of a comparable car with an internal-combustion engine.
>
> Former Toyota President and Chairman Hiroshi Okuda as he increased the fuel-efficiency goal in the middle of developing the gas-electric Prius, which has proven to be a huge competitive advantage for Toyota [14]

Successful BHAGs create corporate capabilities that are difficult, if not impossible, for competitors to copy. Coupled with the "tortoise" of continuous improvement, such a "hare" can help to create sustainable competitive advantage.

All levels of the plan (corporate, divisional, departmental, team, and even individual) must be linked, driven by the same strategy and focused on the same goals. This way, the entire corporate workforce is pulling on the same rope in the same direction. As we'll see in a later chapter, when managers sit down with their people to map out the year ahead, the corporate plan should be in front of them so that each individual's goals can be structured to help achieve departmental, divisional, and corporate goals.

THE WORLD IN YOUR FACE

PLANNING IN A GLOBAL ENVIRONMENT

No matter whether you are a CEO or a team leader, planning is getting harder because the game is continually expanding, the rules are becoming ever more complex, and there are more and more players. There's no longer any place to hide. For example, just because you decide not to market overseas doesn't mean foreign competitors won't get right in your face here at home.

In theory, you engage today's global environment at two points: an inner and an outer ring. The inner ring, the "task" environment, is where your customers, employees, suppliers, distributors, and competitors co-exist, clash, and cooperate. Here, you can put your hands on events and have some control over inputs and outcomes.

The outer ring, however, is composed of economic, sociocultural, technological, demographic, political, legal, and regulatory forces over which you can exert little or no influence but which can hugely impact your business. All you can do is detect them coming over the horizon and attempt to use or survive them as best you can.

THE INNER RING

SUPPLIERS AND DISTRIBUTORS

If you are a manufacturer, two of the most important entities in your task environment are your suppliers and your distributors. The former partially control your product cost and quality by what they supply you and the latter partially determine your customer satisfaction and reputation by how they represent you. You literally are the bologna in the sandwich.

Companies with a shareholder focus often view themselves as first among equals and—when under economic pressure—will beat down supplier and distributor profit margins to protect their quarterly earnings, the stock price, and the executive bonuses tied to these factors. Treating suppliers and distributors badly is short-term thinking that degrades their ability to provide the support the company needs to succeed over the long term. Managers with this sort of approach also might decrease the research and development budget, mortgaging tomorrow's capabilities to feed today's bottom line. If they are in charge for a long time, they can destroy the company.

By contrast, companies with a stakeholder mentality realize that a value chain (supplier> manufacturer > distributor) is simply a coalition of stakeholders cooperating to collectively transform resources into value, satisfy customers, and share the wealth they create. They realize that they cannot succeed if their business partners do not succeed as well. To borrow a phrase from the novelist Alexandre Dumas, "All for one and one for all." [15]

SHAREHOLDER VERSUS STAKEHOLDER

Although the *Fortune* magazine writer might have taken them out of context or I might have given them undue weight, comments by General Electric's Chief Information Officer (CIO) Gary Reiner, who also oversees GE's purchasing and Six Sigma quality assurance programs, exemplify what I believe is wrong with a shareholder, rather than stakeholder, company culture. [16]

In describing GE's purchasing activities, Reiner said, "Our job would be to commoditize the item as much as possible and then leverage IT (information technology) to have our suppliers bid for the business." But speaking of GE's own products, he said, "By design, every year we try to make more of our ... products and services non-commodity ... differentiated." In short, he wants to commoditize GE's input to minimize cost and differentiate GE's output to maximize pricing opportunity.

Obviously, decreasing input cost and increasing output profit will *add* value and fatten GE's bottom line. But will it *maximize* value? Or is it instead a short-term approach that ignores the possibility of enhancing value through increased stakeholder collaboration that provides prosperity to every company in the value chain? Only a more thorough investigation of GE—one of the most successful companies in history—would provide the answer. But Reiner's words conveniently spotlight a key principle of this book. Treating companies providing your input and companies selling your output as truly equal business partners collaborating with you to create value and gain wealth *together* is an approach often used by successful companies with long-term viewpoints.

An example would be Toyota and Honda helping their suppliers to increase their quality and decrease their cost instead of—as GM, Ford, and Chrysler have so often done in the past—simply demanding a price cut regardless of the impact on the supplier. Incidentally, both GM and Ford have recently moved closer to this "value-sharing" practice in their relations with suppliers while Toyota has begun to press suppliers for lower prices.

DEALING WITH COMPETITORS

Your competitors—other companies that provide the same product or service or could do so—also are part of your task environment. Strong competitive rivalry improves quality and technology. Imagine what the product quality of GM, Ford, and Chrysler would be today if Honda, Nissan, and Toyota had not stuck a competitive spur into them.

But, as noted above, competitive rivalry can commoditize products, degrade prices, lower profits, and create mutually assured destruction. Before this stage is reached, it's logical for companies to find ways (industry coalitions, cooperative pre-competitive research, pooled sourcing, or joint-venture manufacturing) to cooperate in cost-reduction and product-enhancement activities. For example, long-time arch rivals Mercedes and BMW are discussing joint parts purchasing and Mercedes recently formed an economy of scale agreement with Renault/Nissan. [17]

Cooperation also can provide pooled financial strength and the magnified political influence necessary to overcome heavy capital investment requirements or government regulations that undercut competitive capability. Note, however, that this sort of cooperation requires the participants to have complete understanding and respect for anti-trust laws and to be willing to be honest with one another—not easy feats.

THE OUTER RING

ECONOMIC, TECHNOLOGY, SOCIOCULTURAL, AND DEMOGRAPHIC FORCES

Other than lobbying your congressmen and senators, there is very little you can do to keep the Fed from raising interest rates, inflating the currency to keep the economy from recession, or nationalizing private companies to avoid financial meltdown. These are examples of economic forces over which you have virtually no control. But you can prepare your company to deal with the likely consequences of these forces in the outer ring. For example:

> Minimize debt and maximize retained earnings so your company has pockets deep enough to ride out today's recession without undercutting its ability to capitalize on tomorrow's rebound. Obviously, deep pockets and liquidity are vital in situations like the current credit crunch. In a recent issue, *The Economist*

noted that DuPont invested heavily in R&D during the Great Depression of the 1930s and succeeded during the post-depression boom because 40 percent of its products (including world-changing nylon and synthetic rubber) were less than ten years old. [18]

Create new technology or track its development by suppliers so that you are better prepared to incorporate it into your products as Toyota and Honda did with the computer technology enabling reliable gas-electric drive-trains.

Track your current customers and realize that age is making their eyes weaker, their fingers stiffer, and their reactions slower, requiring you to accommodate their changed needs with incremental product improvement even as you chase the next generation of younger consumers with product innovation.

Monitor major-market population projections to discover where around the globe you must invest in new manufacturing or distribution capability over the coming decades.

Track political developments in international trade and have what-if plans ready to implement when a new trade agreement presents new opportunities.

If you routinely employ these conservative measures, when a downturn arrives, you will have the knowledge, plans, and resources to outspend, outinvent, outlast and outsmart less-prepared competitors. This will enable you to enhance your brand strength and gain market share, expanding your profits when the next upturn occurs. Retained earnings, a top-tier credit rating, and prudent preparation can combine to form a wonderful competitive advantage.

THE PROMISE AND THREAT OF EVER-EMERGING COMMUNICATION TECHNOLOGY

Technology has made all of this easier to do. Global corporate computer systems operate 24/7 so that your engineers in Japan or Germany use the system while their American colleagues sleep—usually contributing to a shared product development database that can create component sharing and optimize economy of scale. If necessary, you can climb on a plane and be six thousand miles away ten hours later when just sixty years ago, you would have faced a ten-day trip on a ship. Or you can stay in your office and videoconference, e-mail, or telephone your colleagues virtually anytime, anywhere.

While the productivity spur provided by this "always-on" technology cannot be denied, it can have a human cost. A recent study by the Pew Internet & American Life Project examined some of the consequences. According to the *Wall Street Journal*[19]:

- The study considers 96 percent of the US workforce as "wired and ready" with Internet access, e-mail, or cell phone.
- Three out of four in this group say that technology has improved their ability to share ideas.
- And 58 percent say it has made their jobs more flexible.

But there is a downside:

- 49 percent say it makes their job more stressful
- 46 percent say the technology makes them work more hours
- And most of those owning Blackberries never stop working: 70 percent of them check work-related e-mails on the weekend; 55 percent check e-mails on vacation, and 48 percent reveal that they are required to respond to e-mails when not at work. Finally, if you don't temporarily confiscate their equipment, they will do so in your meetings as well.

In short, today's communication technology is seductive, productive, and intrusive—both a convenience and a curse.

Joining the work-addicted Blackberry crowd is a choice with far-reaching consequences for your lifestyle. Your employer will take as much of your time as you are willing to give. Your hours will steadily increase as you climb the management ladder. You will spend more and more time at the office or on the road, get home less often, and bring work with you when you do. One day, as you quietly make another stealthy dawn departure, you'll find your five-year-old asleep on the floor, clutching his blanket and trying to block the door so you can't leave.

PLANNING TOOLS

So, what tools do we put into the "Planning" drawer of the toolbox?

Corporate Culture (DNA): The star on the horizon that defines and guides a company, composed of core ideology (Who are we?), core purpose (Why do we exist?), and the answers to several other questions that follow.

The four foundation questions begin the planning process: 1) What is our product or service? 2) Who will buy it? 3) What do they want? 4) How can we give it to them in ways that . . . ?

Mission: Why are we here? Best answered with a succinct, inspiring statement designed to fill all employees with urgent purpose and point them in the same direction.

Values: What do we hold most dear?

Vision: Where are we going?

Strategy: How will we get there?

Goals: Targets that comprise the focus of the company's strategy. They must be clearly defined before success can be achieved and measured with key performance indicators (KPIs), which will be discussed in following sections of this book.

The planning loop: The corporate-wide communication process that directs values, vision, mission, and strategy (VVMS) *down* the corporate hierarchy and asks for suggested improvements, tactics, timetables, and resource requests to come back *up*. This "loop" process creates shared understanding and ownership of the plan from top to bottom and aligns, commits and energizes the organization to execute it.

SWOT: Classical planning analysis technique composed of four questions: 1) What are our strengths? 2) What are our weaknesses? 3) What opportunities are available in the business environment? 4) What threats face us?

The three Rs: Responsibilities, Resources, and Results; in order to create and achieve a corporate plan, you *define the first, grant the second, and demand the third.*

Benchmarking: Examining other companies to see what useful improvements you can adopt or adapt

Bracketing: The planning practice of composing 1) best-case, 2) likely-case, and 3) worst-case plans so that the company is relatively ready for all envisioned "futures." Most companies implement the likely case.

Crisis Planning: Establishing a standing crisis committee, anticipating various potential incidents, and constructing fairly detailed "just-in-case" plans for each so that the company is prepared to react quickly if one of the scenarios suddenly comes crashing through the boardroom wall.

Commoditizing: A destructive process resulting from intense competition. It erodes product uniqueness, making your products interchangeable with competitors' products in customers' minds and denying producers the opportunity to differentiate themselves and their offerings from one another. The usual result is overproduction, falling prices, and failing companies that chase the same customers with increasingly similar products and processes. But the customers are happy. Avoid it by building brand strength that can help create sustainable competitive advantage (easy to say but hard to do).

Linkage: Assuring that plans at all levels in the company (corporate, divisional, department, team, individual) are linked and aimed at the same goals, causing everyone to pull on the same rope in the same direction.

PDCA (plan, do, check, act): Plan it, do it, check the results against the targets, improve the process to narrow the gap, and then do it over and over and over to achieve …

Kaizen: The powerfully competitive "tortoise" of *continuous improvement,* which combined with …

BHAG: A *big hairy audacious goal* that creates new corporate capability can achieve …

Sustainable Competitive Advantage: A unique combination of vision, strategy, and capabilities difficult, if not impossible, to copy—consigning competitors forever to second place.

Run Scared: What the British troops at Islandlwana did not do but what smart, well-managed companies always do. Any plan these companies decide to execute has a built-in margin of safety.

Certainty: What planners (and managers of any kind) long for but will never possess. Time, cost, and capability always limit information-gathering activities. Consequently, you will never have *perfect knowledge* before you must decide among competing courses of action. Good planning can minimize risk, but eventually the pressure of circumstances will push you into placing a carefully considered bet.

Feelings and Facts: The two "F" words. Good planners tend to downplay the first and embrace the second. Our second president, John Adams, called facts "stubborn things." [20] Another bright politician, the late U.S Senator from New York, Daniel Patrick Moynihan, said, "You are entitled to your own opinions, but not your own facts." [21] Feelings are both unavoidable and vital. Brain research clearly demonstrates that our emotions affect every action we take, helping to shape and drive both personal and corporate decisions. They are absolutely necessary to honesty; integrity; ethics; and authentic, connected leadership—particularly during a crisis. But facts are where intelligent people can most easily find the day-to-day common ground necessary to agree on a course of action. *Facts* drive the planning that precedes decision-making. *Find them, analyze them, use them.*

The planner's mind: Good planners are knowledge-hungry, fact-driven, skeptical, paranoid, aware of their limitations, and intensely curious. Many of them start every day with the same two questions: "What has changed?" and "What are the short- and long-term implications of the change for my company?" All of this helps make them good managers. Even if they are not familiar with it, they also believe in the command summarized by the Japanese term *genchi genbutsu* (go and see) because *firsthand* experience always tops *secondhand* reports.

All of these characteristics coalesce in an ability to perceive patterns, opportunities, and threats in ambiguous and sometimes contradictory information. When you combine the planner's mentality, these tools, and disciplined operational techniques designed to harvest resources for re-investment in value creation, you create a very powerful management system. But we need to add one final tool.

A LESSON FROM GENERAL MOTORS

The final and most important tool in the planning drawer is the what-if game. What better place to determine the need for this vital tool than General Motors.

As I began writing this book, GM—once America's biggest company—was sliding rapidly towards bankruptcy while my management students tracked its glide path. As usual, I had divided them into teams and asked each team to prepare and deliver a fifteen-minute power point presentation answering these questions:

- Using the principles taught in this course, explain how GM went wrong and identify the "root" cause for its unfolding failure.
- Is it too late for GM to recover? What measures would you recommend to restore it to fully competitive condition?

- Was the government wise to bail out GM?

Although they have identified and described many symptoms and suggested some good remedies over the years, only a few of the student teams have fully captured the root cause of GM's downfall: *a proud and powerful corporate culture that prevented management from asking, "What if?" and then taking timely and aggressive action to change the company's future.*

GM celebrated its hundredth birthday in 2008. During its first sixty years, it became America's biggest company and the world's biggest automaker. But then the rules of competition that had enabled its success began to change. The membership of US labor unions declined even as their demands continued to rise. Foreign-owned competitors established productive, lower-cost, non-union operations in the southern US and their high-quality fuel-efficient products—particularly cars—became very popular.

These and other factors made the Detroit automakers ever more dependent on profit from big, thirsty trucks and sport utility vehicles (SUVs). The cost of energy began to creep up in the US and became very expensive in most other major markets. The unique nature of the energy-intensive American market hampered GM's efforts to use the same vehicle "platforms" in all major markets while Japanese automakers were able to achieve cost-saving economies of scale with their fuel-efficient, globe-girdling product platforms (until they ventured into large trucks and SUVs).

While GM's market share slowly shrank, successive generations of management failed to ask the right questions and take sufficiently aggressive actions:

- What if competitors offer products that are lower-cost and higher-quality than ours? For a long time, GM was blind to this even as it happened.
- What if foreign automakers achieve dominance in the US car market?
- What if they continue to establish North American manufacturing operations that are more productive, lower-cost, and more flexible than ours?
- What if we end up with too many unprofitable or marginally profitable dealers unable to represent us properly and virtually impossible to get rid of?
- What if eight different brands stretch our resources too far, forcing us to turn out increasingly generic and unattractive products differentiated only by their nameplates and not supported by sufficient marketing resources.
- What if the cost of the overly generous medical and retirement benefits we have granted in a vain effort to buy labor peace make each vehicle we build significantly more expensive to manufacture than similar foreign-nameplate products?
- What if global demand for oil drastically accelerates, driving the price of gas up and buyers out of trucks and SUVs? Note that this is the key question my colleagues and I should have asked each other as we con-

sidered recommending the Texas truck plant to the Toyota board of directors.

- What if our foreign competitors succeed with the fuel-efficient, gas-electric "hybrid" technology we initially rejected?
- What if we get deeply into debt, a sudden financial crisis restricts credit, and a sales crash chokes off our cash flow?

Hindsight is always wise. But while most of these circumstances materialized slowly over decades, a more curious and fact-driven corporate culture (see "planner's mind" above) would have noted the trends and reacted much more quickly and aggressively. A less insular culture also might have been more open to life-saving change.

GENERAL MOTORS → GENEROUS MOTORS → GOVERNMENT MOTORS

The philosopher and essayist George Santayana once said, "Those who cannot remember the past, are condemned to repeat it." [22] The US government (and several other governments for their "national" automakers) proved him right by bailing out GM and Chrysler with taxpayer money and facilitating quick bankruptcies for both.

The US government is not the first to believe it can forestall the inevitable by rewarding failure. British Leyland Motor Corporation (BLMC) was formed in 1968 from the wreckage of England's "native" auto industry.

The firm's primary nameplates were Jaguar, Rover, Land Rover, and Mini.

BLMC was unsuccessful for the first six years it existed. Then, in 1975, the British government stepped in to "save" the company and its "jobs" by creating a new, partially nationalized entity with the government as a prominent shareholder. Does this sound familiar?

After several reorganizations and huge losses over the next thirty years, British Leyland—by then called the MG Rover Group—declared bankruptcy, taking taxpayer money and private-sector debt down the drain. Rover is gone. Jaguar and Land Rover are owned by the Indian automaker Tata. Mini is owned by BMW. And there is no "native" British-owned auto industry. Nevertheless, 1.65 million motor vehicles were produced in the United Kingdom in 2007 under new ownership—all foreign (Ford, GM, Toyota, Honda, Nissan, et al). As the late Ronald Reagan once observed, "Government does not solve problems. It subsidizes them." [23]

THINGS TO THINK ABOUT

- Is it sensible for government to use tariffs, financial bailouts, nationalization, and other measures to try to protect "jobs"? Are protectionism and subsidies the best way for a country to remain competitive? Is there a down side to such "beggar-thy-neighbor" policies?

- Is it wise for any government to use laws and regulations to hinder the free flow of capital, labor, and manufacturing to the most efficient uses and locations, even if they are in countries other than the US? What unanticipated problems could this strategy cause?

- For a long time, GM's nickname was "Generous Motors" because of the many excellent benefits—particularly subsidized healthcare and pensions—it provided. The cost of those benefits eventually added more than $1,300 to the suggested retail price of each vehicle GM produced—a huge disadvantage. How could this situation have been avoided?

Unlike GM and BLMC, good corporate planners realize that success depends upon continuously adapting to inevitable change. Management theory and practices also have changed over the years. Here in America, they have evolved within a free-enterprise economy based on a laissez-faire foundation. Let's briefly look at the primary roots of free enterprise—as well as the objections of its most persuasive and influential critic—and see how today's American management methods reflect them.

To do so, I'll briefly introduce you to a royal bureaucrat, four economists, and nine experts who made substantial and unique contributions to management theory. Although others were involved, these people represent the most significant steppingstones along the path that has led to today's predominant American corporate culture and structure.

JEAN-BAPTISTE COLBERT (1619–1683)

Colbert was the French finance minister from 1665 to 1683 under King Louis XIV, who liked to fight expensive wars. Colbert heavily taxed the French people to pay for them.

He is said to have said, "The art of taxation consists in so plucking the goose as to obtain the largest amount of feathers with the least amount of hissing." Colbert also is credited with causing the creation of the term *laissez faire* when, during a 1680 meeting, he asked a group of successful French businessmen what he and the government could do for them. They supposedly answered, "Laissez-nous faire!" which roughly translates to "Leave us be!" Little did any of the participants know that this term would become the rallying cry for free enterprise where outcomes are determined more by the market than by the government. [1] Let's look at some of the experts who helped to create this market-based system.

ECONOMISTS WHO LAID CAPITALISM'S FOUNDATION

ADAM SMITH (1723–90)

Adam Smith was a Scottish moral philosopher often referred to as the "father of modern economics." His most important economic theory (stated in his seminal 1776 book *The Wealth of Nations)* was that the unintended consequence of each individual's pursuit of rational self-interest in a free-market economy is the creation of wealth and value that benefits society as a whole. He called this the "invisible hand." His most important contribution to management theory was the concept of division of labor. Smith noted that companies manufactured pins in one of two ways: *craft style* where each worker did all steps to manufacture a single pin, and *divided style* where each worker specialized in a single step of the production process. He pointed out that the "division of labor" in the latter approach resulted in many more pins each day because each worker became expert at his step, multiplying productivity. An unintended consequence was the stimulation of structure to coordinate the activities of the now divided workers. [2]

DAVID RICARDO (1772-1823)

Ricardo became successful and wealthy in real estate and the stock market, enabling him to retire at the age of forty-two. He read Smith's *Wealth of Nations* in 1799 and developed an abiding interest in economics that fueled his own writings on the subject. His major work is *Principles of Political Economy and Taxation,* which introduced, among other things, the concept of "comparative advantage" that underlies international trade. Ricardo held that by specializing in what it produced most cost effectively and trading with other countries for other goods, each country, its trading partners, and the global trade system as a whole would prosper. [3]

JOSEPH SCHUMPETER (1883-1950)

Schumpeter, who spent the last eighteen years of his life teaching at Harvard, was an Austrian economist best known for analyzing business cycles and the impact of entrepreneurship. In his book *The Theory of Economic Development,* he describes the disruptive and renewing effects of entrepreneurial innovation. Calling the process "the perennial gale of creative destruction," he noted that the destruction of ineffective old products by more effective new ones is a prime driver of capitalist economies. If—in the name of saving "jobs"—an economy prevents this destruction/creation process from functioning freely, the economy can stagnate and fail. I believe that today's US economy is courting these dangerous consequences. [4]

JOHN MAYNARD KEYNES (1883-1946)

Probably the most influential economist of the twentieth century, Keynes would be supportive of government's current intervention in the market. His ideas are the very antithesis of the free-market economists. In his 1936 book *General Theory of Employment, Interest and Money,* he advocates massive government-provided stimulus in order to energize a falling economy by overcoming the "stickiness" that prevents the full and free functioning of supply and demand. [5]

I could have added other influential economists to this brief summary. Ludwig von Mises (1881–1973), Arthur Pigou (1877–1959), Friedrich von Hayek (1899–1992) and Milton Friedman (1912–2006) come readily to mind. They disagreed with Keynes on the central economic question of government versus market control of the economy. As noted above, Keynes advocated government intervention to stimulate demand. Von Mises, Hayek, and Friedman were against major, direct government involvement in the economy. Pigou also was except for "spillover" problems with a significant "social cost" not governed by the market but instead requiring government intervention. The "heirs of Adam Smith" (as John Cassidy calls them in his latest book, *How Markets Fail),* advocated dependence on an unfettered, self-correcting market where supply and demand could automatically assure efficient use of resources, fair pricing, economic freedom, and prosperity. As we'll see later in this book, this approach requires top corporate executives to balance and control self-interest with ethical and responsible behavior. Like most things in life, the truth probably lies somewhere between Keynes and his critics, but the argument is ongoing and the current U.S. administration is applying massive "stimulation" to our economy that could have very negative long-term consequences.

NINE NINJAS OF MANAGEMENT THEORY

FREDERICK W. TAYLOR (1856-1915)

Frederick Winslow Taylor, an American mechanical engineer, is often called the "father of scientific management." Building on Smith's division of labor, he developed his management philosophy while rising to chief engineer of the Midvale Steel Works in Pennsylvania. Taylor emphasized optimizing the *process.* Carrying a stopwatch and a clipboard, he studied the time and motion of manufacturing processes, altering them to determine the most efficient method, which he then codified with written operating procedures and standards. Then he selected the best workers, trained them to carry out the procedure, and enforced his "one best way," greatly increasing productivity. But the downside was worker boredom and disaffection. Taylor brought his methods to Ford Motor Company in its early years. Management misused Taylor's methods to dehumanize workers, treating them like cogs in a relentless machine, "hands" with no "brains." [6]

HENRI FAYOL (1842–1925)

In his 1917 book *General and Industrial Management,* Fayol defined the main functions of management, a definition still substantially unchanged today (planning, leading, organizing, commanding, and controlling—commanding has since been dropped).

Fayol noted that his view of management was "top down" while Taylor's was "bottom up." His was a broad and complete philosophy of operational management as opposed to Taylor's functional approach. Fayol extracted fourteen desirable management principles from his management functions: 1) specialization of labor, 2) authority, 3) discipline, 4) unity of command, 5) unity of direction, 6) subordination of individual interests, 7) fair remuneration, 8) centralization, 9) clear chain of command from top to bottom, 10) order (everyone in their proper place), 11) even-handed treatment, 12) limited turnover of personnel, 13) individual initiative, and 14) esprit de corps ("harmonious cohesion"). [7]

MAX WEBER (1864-1920)

Maximilian Carl Emil Weber was a German political economist and sociologist considered one of the founders of the study of sociology and public administration. Webber's studies ranged over a broad spectrum of subjects. He popularized the term bureaucracy with his studies of the sociology of government administration.

Applying his observations to business, Weber noted that: 1) a manager's formal authority should derive from his position in the organization; 2) position should be based on competence and performance, not connections and social standing; 3) each position's responsibilities and relationships to other positions should be clearly specified; 4) positions should be arranged hierarchically from the top down, and 5) clearly defined, well-understood rules, procedures, and norms should govern organizational actions. His observations described the many-layered, command-and-control organizations typical of the early to mid-twentieth century. [8]

ELTON MAYO (1880-1949)

Elton Mayo was an Austrian psychologist and sociologist who spent most of his career at the Harvard Business School. The founder of the human relations movement, Mayo probably is best known for the Hawthorne Studies conducted at a Western Electric plant in Cicero, Illinois in the 1930s. The study was intended to determine the effects of improved lighting upon productivity. Instead, it discovered that workers reacted favorably to the attention paid to them and productivity increased. Lighting had nothing to do with it. [9]

ABRAHAM MASLOW (1908–1970)

Abraham Maslow was an American psychologist noted for defining a "hierarchy" of human needs. His unhappy childhood ("I was the only little Jewish boy in a non-Jewish neighborhood; like being the first Negro in an all-white school.") might have influenced his desire to understand human motivation. Maslow viewed human needs as a ladder of motivation beginning at the bottom with air, water, food, and sex. Next came safety needs such as security and stability. Psychological and social needs such as being accepted and loved made up the next rung. At the top were needs for self-actualization—"to be all that you can be," as the US Army puts it, and to make a contribution to something bigger than yourself. [10]

DOUGLAS MCGREGOR (1906–1964)

Douglas McGregor was a psychologist and management professor at MIT's Sloan School of Management and later president of Antioch College. In his 1960 book *The Human Side of Enterprise,* he proposed two theories of management called theories X and Y. Theory X held that the average human being inherently dislikes work and must be threatened and controlled before he will work hard enough. In contrast, theory Y held that the average human being will seek self-fulfillment through work if management creates the proper conditions. Although he stated that practical management is likely to require some combination of the two approaches, McGregor believed that the firms of his day were not getting top performance from their workers because they underestimated their capabilities, creativity and initiative. [11]

W. EDWARDS DEMING (1900–1993)

Deming was a leader in applying statistical process control to improve efficiency, effectiveness, and product quality. He learned the basic techniques from Dr. Walter Shewhart during an internship in 1927 at the Bell Telephone Laboratories while working on his PhD at Yale. When he began to develop his methods in the 1950s, Deming was ignored by American management interested only in quantity, not quality. So he moved to Japan to work with the Japanese Union of Scientists and Engineers (JUSE). Japanese corporate management was so receptive to Deming's quality-improvement techniques that JUSE named its leading quality award the Deming Prize. Deming emphasized long-term commitment to a total system of continuous improvement based on a teaching-learning corporate culture. Deming also stressed that quality cannot be inspected-in at the end of the line, but instead must be built-in on the line. I was privileged to be a junior participant in a few of the plant visits he made while consulting for Ford Motor Company in the early 1980s. [12]

PETER DRUCKER (1909–2005)

Peter Drucker was one of the most prolific and well-known management experts, authors, and consultants to companies and governments in the twentieth century. Born in Vienna, he grew up in a household full of discussion and discovery. His father, a lawyer, was friends with some of Austria's leading intellectuals, including Joseph Schumpeter. Drucker earned his doctorate in international law from the University of Frankfurt in 1931. He concluded his illustrious career at Claremont Graduate University in California where the business school is named after him. As the Nazi party began its rise to power in 1933, he fled Germany to London, where he married Doris Schmitz in 1934. They relocated to the US shortly after the wedding. The first of Drucker's many books, *Concept of the Corporation,* was published in 1944. It was based on a two-year study of the management principles and practices at General Motors, which opened its doors to him. GM Chairman Alfred Sloan considered the book hypercritical. Drucker focused on the relationships between people and how to use management skills to bring out the best in them. Many of what he believed to be effective management concepts and practices are highlighted in this book. [13]

WILLIAM OUCHI (1943 -)

Ouchi, a professor at UCLA, described theory Z—a management method formed by melding Japanese and American styles—in his 1981 book *Theory Z: How American Management Can Meet the Japanese Challenge.* Its primary principles include:

- Individual responsibility combined with cross-functional teams
- Collective, consensual decision-making
- Implicit, informal control with explicit formalized performance measures

- Slow evaluation and promotion, long-term employment and high job security
- Moderate specialization; worker learns all aspects of the operation [14]

THE RESULTS: MANAGEMENT AND STRUCTURAL EVOLUTION

The findings of Mayo, Maslow, McGregor, Deming, Drucker, and Ouchi completed the evolution from a focus solely on process to one on people as well. This laid the foundation of the humanistic school of psychology and accelerated developments resulting in today's team-oriented organizational methods. Management methods and corporate structure have evolved from: process → people + process; totalitarian → team; command → consensus and collaboration; tall and rigid → flat, flexible and fast.

As we'll see in the next section, today's adaptable corporate structures are based on cross-organizational teamwork driving horizontal customer-satisfaction processes through vertical organizational silos in order to foster fast, effective communication; broad sharing of actionable information; distributed leadership; and collaborative decision-making. Whew! Quite a mouthful, isn't it? But you'll get it. Trust me.

ELEPHANTS CAN'T DANCE

Successful companies realize that change is the only constant and they can succeed only by destroying the parts of their past that are no longer relevant and using the rescued resources to create their future.

The ideal corporate structure to match this reality would be a single cell that automatically adjusts its shape to changing circumstances, reacting swiftly and consistently no matter where it is touched. Unfortunately, no one has yet figured out how to create such a perfectly adaptive organization. Instead, being human, we tend to do the opposite. Most of us long for predictable stability. And so we try to impose order and deny or decelerate change by categorizing and filing everything, including each other.

In most American corporations, for example, we house people doing similar jobs in little towers, wire each tower with a clear chain of command, and provide rules telling everyone what to expect and what is expected. Then we stack all the little towers up into a multi-tiered pyramid with an expensive, all-powerful CEO standing on top, pointing toward *his* true north and bellowing, "Follow me!"

We need a quick, intelligent amoeba. But if we follow our natural tendencies, we create an elephant. *And elephants can't dance!*

This sort of corporate structure is inflexible, slow to react, resistant to change, and often like a large oak with too many branches and rotten roots. It projects strength but cannot stand up to the winds of change. Unfortunately, at least some of it also is necessary. However, tools and techniques we will discuss in this section can make it react more efficiently, effectively, and quickly to the pull of the marketplace.

But let's review first. Remember the four basic business foundation questions from the planning chapter?

- What is our product or service?
- Who will buy it?
- What do they want in the product, sales, and service process?
- How can we give it to them in ways that will energize us, differentiate us from competitors, capture customer loyalty, make money, and build sustainable competitive advantage?

Finding customers; satisfying their desires (even those they don't yet know they have); and building lasting, profitable relationships with them are the basic goals of all business. The way an organization is structured and motivated can help or hamper efforts to do so.

A certain amount of structure is necessary; but, like government, less is best. Here's why. In addition to being centralized, traditional corporate structure tends to be *vertical.* Grouping people with similar skills and functions into departments makes it easier for them to work with and learn from one another inside their department and for managers to oversee their activities. But like the tide, the market's pull is *horizontal,* requiring these different departmental silos to overcome the *insularity of similarity* and link their activities in order to provide what customers want when, where, and how they want it. Successful companies have learned to react to the horizontal tug of the market quickly, efficiently, and accurately. How do they do it?

Think of market demand as a series of ropes. A customer demands something by tugging on one end of a rope. The retailer on the rope's other end feels the tug with his left hand and, in turn, tugs on the rope in his right hand, connecting him to you, the producer. You feel the tug with your left hand and tug on the ropes in your right hand, connecting you to your key suppliers. They, in turn, tug on the ropes connecting them to their suppliers. Except for the customer, everyone in this demand chain tugs only when tugged upon and production begins only when the customer-initiated tug reaches the far end of the chain.

No company ever fully achieves this idealized *just-in-time* "pull" system. Many factors can kink the ropes. But, as we'll see in the section on "Controlling," even compromised versions can minimize the waste and expense of stockpiling "just-in-case" resources within the system by activating production in response to genuine customer "pull," not in response to the "push" of costly, underutilized manufacturing capacity.

In a traditionally structured company, the departmental silos with their layered verticality create a series of walls that can interrupt and slow down response to this horizontal tugging. The cost of creating, staffing, and maintaining the silos also tempts companies to book a profit by producing and pushing inventory and cost onto retailers, regardless of true market demand.

In addition to being expensive, these silos also can slow decision-making and scramble communication by forcing both into a vertical, up-and-down pattern centered on top management. But as business has gone global, competition hyper, and communication electronic, corporate structure has been forced to evolve to meet the constantly increasing need for faster, more accurate reaction to the outside environment and to overcome the growing challenge of constantly improving competitors—in short, to more efficiently and effectively deal with the expanding and evolving tug of the market.

However, management still needs to see over the walls and be seen by employees in order to control, coordinate, unify, and lead them. Furthermore, the expertise, experience, and skills housed in the departmental silos need to be effectively brought to bear on the company's processes to assure quality, improve productivity, enforce consistency, and control costs.

Creating a structure that allows control, collaboration, market sensitivity, and quick reaction to smoothly mesh rather than clash is a balancing act. Furthermore, it's different for each company and each set of circumstances. And finally, the structure must continuously evolve in step with the external environment, which crosses new borders every day. Wow! It's global, three-dimensional chess.

In order to win this game, you must create a *learning* organization that can:

- Adapt quickly to the changing external environment
- Foster creative collaboration, clear and quick communication, and accurate decision-making
- Coordinate and focus "silo" expertise to satisfy customers more efficiently and effectively than competitors
- And react rapidly and consistently no matter where demand tugs on it

As we will see, the primary tools to achieve this are goal-setting, teamwork, control/motivational systems, and corporate culture.

Note that structure might be hybrid in order to meet different needs within the organization. For example, production activities might require structure intolerant of mistakes and waste in order to assure quality and enforce cost control. But the same "justify-the-cost" approach would smother a research and development department needing to explore likely opportunities that can turn out to be expensive blind alleys. As I already noted, balancing discipline and creativity is one of the key functions of good management.

Furthermore, a company might go through organizational phases. As it grows from local to regional to national to international to global, it might evolve from a product setup with structure devoted to each product line to, for example, a setup with structure devoted to all business within a certain geographical area such as North

America or Europe. This regional setup describes Toyota today, but it began as a national company that initially served its overseas markets with Japan-built products.

Or a conglomerate might adopt a company-within-a-company approach where individual divisions dedicated to each type of business regularly report results (KPIs) to a small central "corporate" staff that tracks performance and enforces cost control, market focus, and a uniform culture.

Continually advancing computer technology (data gathering/storage/analysis, swift/broad sharing of information, and instant-global-24/7 communication) has facilitated the development of flat, flexible, reactive "learning" organizations with geographically dispersed operations. But thinner control structure—fewer managers with broader spans of control—and more expansive access to actionable information also empower employees, requiring a new framework and rigorous training to guide their decision-making when close, day-to-day supervision is no longer possible.

COMPANIES COME IN ALL SIZES

Because of my background, I have focused on the organizational practices and pitfalls of large corporations. But there are many more small companies than large. How do you organize your own business?

Among the smaller forms you can use before resorting to a full corporation are a sole proprietorship, a partnership, a limited liability company, and an S corporation. Which one you pick depends on your desired combination of privacy, flexibility, tax benefits, and shielding against personal liability for company debts.

For example, a sole proprietorship has only one stockholder (you) with all the privacy and flexibility that implies. But you pay personal tax on the company's profits, and your personal assets can be seized to pay off company liabilities. In a limited liability company, you can have an unlimited number of shareholders, the tax benefits are similar to a partnership, and your personal assets are shielded from company liability.

You might start your company as a sole proprietorship and evolve into one of the other forms over time. But large or small, you still will need to hire the best people you can afford, minimize the cost of added structure, and create a strong "compass" culture as your company grows beyond your ability to run it in a personal, hands-on fashion.

GROWTH REQUIRES CULTURE CREATION AND TRAINING

Well-known restaurateur Danny Meyer faced these imperatives when his company grew beyond the very successful Union Square Café into a company with hundreds of employees working at eleven well-known and successful New York City eating establishments. How do you extend success beyond your small start without expanding into bankruptcy? In his book *Setting the Table*, Meyer puts it this way. "I managed by example, and I had yet to learn how critically important it is to lead by teaching, setting priorities, and holding people accountable." 1

In other words, when you can no longer be there to directly control and assure performance by saying, "Watch and do what I do," you need goals, operating procedures, a clear and compelling corporate culture, and lots of training to do it for you. And that means you will have to create structure to set the goals, train your people, assure follow-up, and reward high performance.

DESIGNING EFFECTIVE STRUCTURE

Whether it's a small or large company, part of your managerial function will be job design—dividing tasks into specific jobs that will best achieve organizational goals by simplifying, enlarging, or enriching responsibility. Another part will be designing structure to group employees with similar functions and responsibilities into departments and then figuring out how to breach the walls between the departments to create the cross-organizational communication and collaboration (horizontal *tugging*) that satisfies customers.

As stated above, departmental benefits include learning from others doing similar jobs and ease of monitoring and control for management. But unintended consequences can include the silo effect that scrambles communication, inhibits interdepartmental cooperation, and blocks sight of the big corporate picture.

The usual solution is cross-departmental teams composed of members who bring "silo" expertise to the table.

These teams focus on satisfying the "pull" of customer demand to achieve corporate goals. For example, most automakers assure the effective focusing of silo expertise (sales, product development, chassis engineering, body engineering, engine engineering, manufacturing engineering, etc.) on meeting market pull by using cross-functional product teams.

At Toyota North America, the management of the Camry team consists of a Japanese chief engineer, an American executive engineer, a manufacturing engineer, and a product planner from the sales department to represent customer needs and desires. When a new Camry is introduced, the team members are immediately out in the market, assessing acceptance and picking up reaction from dealers and customers to feed into the next Camry, the planning of which usually starts immediately.

TEAMWORK

Why are teams effective? Because they have *more* of everything than someone working alone: more brains, more resources, more knowledge of the pieces and parts of the organization, more understanding of the marketplace, and more diversity of viewpoint. They link the collective, collaborative, creative brainpower of the silos and focus it to achieve organizational goals. They also enable employees to feel they are part of something bigger than themselves, which increases job satisfaction. But teams will do all of this only if they are managed properly. Here are some suggestions.

When forming and managing a team:

- Pick busy people because they know how to get things done.
- Make sure each team has a full deck of cards by picking people with complementary skills.
- Keep teams relatively small—no more than seven to nine members so that no one can hide from individual responsibility and discussion and decisions are more easily conducted and reached. When necessary, supplement with temporary members who leave when their task is done.
- Reward both individual and team performance with, for example, a two-bonus system. (You get what you reward.)
- Clearly link team goals to corporate targets, give members the training and tools they need, set a date for final results, and get out of the way.
- Monitor and lead from a distance with a light hand, stepping in to coach—not command—only when necessary.

When you are a team member:

- Organize the meetings if you have to, but never hold one without an agenda and some advance preparations by participants. To do so usually invites a time-wasting bull session.

- Check your ego at the door, but make sure everyone's role and responsibilities are understood and work to assure that everyone's viewpoint is heard and respected. Some Toyota people have called this approach the "Three C" system: consideration, communication, and cooperation.

- Try to keep discussion moving on track. Politely interrupt "dominators" and ask non-participators what they think. Get all the viewpoints out on the table for discussion.

- Be the last to offer ideas so you have the benefit of everyone else's. Then sum up: "Let me see if I understood everyone's ideas…" This enables you to state the meeting's outcome, a powerful role.

Teamwork is a way to breach the walls and bridge the gaps; but traditional structure still is necessary, and it needs to be clear and easily understandable. Each organization requires a chain of command, specifying each manager's relative authority (the power to hold people responsible for their actions and to decide how and when organizational resources are used) and the span of that authority, how many people or departments report to each manager.

Traditional structures are tall with many levels of authority and narrow spans of control. As noted above, this can slow decision-making by separating it from implementation and forcing it upward in the organization. It also is expensive.

To gain speed, today's corporate structures tend to have fewer and wider levels that combine decision-making and execution rather than separating them. But this can decentralize and diffuse control, possibly diluting shared focus and unity of purpose. Broad spans of control also can overload and burn out managers responsible for them.

In addition to teams, the answer is a strong, clear, positive corporate culture and lots of training so that every employee knows how to make decisions that reflect the company's values, vision, strategy, mission, and goals. Assuring the propagation and continuous improvement of this sort of "compass" culture during periods of swift international growth can be difficult, a problem Toyota currently faces.

One way to avoid creating expensive structure (particularly important in cyclical industries where structure added during booms drags during busts) is to use strategic alliances in which two or more firms share technology development or jointly own and operate a production venture. Taken to its extreme, this approach yields a "virtual" company that owns nothing, instead outsourcing all its activities to free-standing entities, which it coordinates.

HOW TO RUN WHAT YOU'VE BUILT

Running the structure you have built is no different than any other business process. You begin with questions. For example:

- Have we selected the right goals?
- Is our process and product quality high?

- Are we measuring success properly?
- Are we turning inputs into outputs efficiently?
- Are we encouraging innovation or simply incentivizing mediocrity?
- Are we making enough money to continually reinvest, increasing our competitive edge?

Depending on the answers you get, apply controls to alter the outcomes. The controls can be:

- Feed-forward (anticipate problems and put controls in place to prevent them)
- Concurrent (correct problems as they arise)
- Feedback (assess results—with a customer satisfaction survey, for example—and take corrective measures)

In any case, you must pay close attention to what measurements define success because, as management expert Peter Drucker said, "What gets measured gets done." [2]

So measure the right things.

As we'll see, your managers must participate in this definition process because the selected criteria become the key performance indicators (KPIs) they must meet. You compare their results to the mutually selected goals and quantify the gap. Then you jointly decide with each manager what corrective actions will narrow or close it. These could include less difficult KPI's, more training, better tools, a different approach, more investment, a different structure, more effort, or a different person.

You also must be careful to provide some flexibility in goal-setting and KPI creation. If you set the bar too high or maintain goals that become unrealistic because external circumstances have deteriorated, employees might cheat to meet them or quit to escape them. This is another reason for always keeping one eye cocked out the window to watch the weather.

And you must focus on the desired time horizon. For example, if you want steady, long-term gain in market share, you would not want to curtail R and D investment in order to fatten short-term profits.

One descriptive term for this goal-setting process is management by objectives (MBO), a phrase coined by Drucker. You sit down with your direct reports one at a time just before the company's fiscal year begins to review their achievements and agree on their individual goals for the coming year. You meet with them periodically during the year to discuss progress. At year end, you base their merit raises, bonuses, and promotions on performance against the mutually agreed goals. As Drucker might have said, "You get the performance you reward."

As discussed in the planning section, the resulting evolutionary change or kaizen is part of the PDCA process in which feedback controls provide the information to construct feed-forward controls, completing the never-ending cycle driving continuous improvement. If you do it in a disciplined way, over time, you create a continuously evolving organization that stays in step with the changing marketplace so you never have to blow it up and start over.

STARTING OVER

But what if you become part of an undisciplined company that has failed to pursue continuous improvement or made unrealistic long-term commitments it cannot keep? It might then become necessary to resort to *revolutionary* change, which has been compared to changing all four tires while the car is going seventy miles an hour.

Crises can take many forms. Frequently, they seem to explode suddenly into existence. Most appear to result from an operational failure. But if you dig deeply enough, you are likely to find that the hidden root cause of most crises has been growing for some time. Usually, it is failure to consistently use PDCA to adapt or failure to play the what-if game that enables a company to react quickly when an alternate reality comes crashing in.

Most crises require revolutionary change that is rapid, bold, and dramatic. They might require you to fire people, outsource work, and sell assets. It's likely that they will require the quick development of new ways of doing things. This requires a strong and charismatic leader who can convince stakeholders that big, swift changes are required and effectively communicate a persuasive and inspiring vision of what—with strong, quick, coordinated effort—the organization can become.

Revolutionary change will use many elements of the standard planning process already described. But usually, too little attention is given to the persuasive leadership skills required to convince people to change.

Leaders in a PDCA company subtly exercise low-key control from the back row in the form of observation, support, coaching, and questioning. This sort of fact-driven planning is the core of effective managing. But in times of crisis, it must be combined with passionate, authentic, emotional communication that will break through the complacent "business-as-usual" attitude to make the quick gut-wrenching changes that will enable the company to survive. This requires a leader who can combine the rational and the emotional in a "come-with-me-to-the-mountaintop" pitch that emotionally connects.

Good communicators intuitively realize that inspiring and persuasive communication relies on storytelling. Before humans learned to write things down, we preserved our history by orally passing stories and allegories from generation to generation. Our hard-wiring still makes us particularly open to this sort of communication.

That's why successful politicians scatter stories through their speeches. Ronald Reagan was very skillful at using stories and humor to persuade others to follow him. I read somewhere that Tip O'Neil, a Democrat and the house majority leader during part of Reagan's eight years as president, would go into the oval office angry and scowling only to emerge thirty minutes later, laughing and sometimes persuaded to remain neutral or slightly cooperative toward something Reagan wanted to get done. The Irish heritage they shared probably helped.

But let's be clear. Too often, the need for emotional communication and rapid, disruptive change is created by bad management practices. The purpose of *revolutionary* change is to restore an organization to a state where *evolutionary* change can be reinstated. If the proper PDCA methods—and the continuous incremental improvement they create—had been diligently used to begin with, a revolution might not be necessary. *The continuous improvement produced by sound, conservative corporate planning, and disciplined execution is the firmest possible foundation for long-term business success.*

HUMAN RESOURCES MANAGEMENT

If you get a job at a medium to large company with a professionally staffed human resources (HR) department, thank whatever god you pray to for making your managerial life easier.

A top-notch HR department creates a system of processes and practices for recruiting, training, and motivating employees that will help assure productivity, quality, and responsiveness to customers. Essentially, the HR department recruits, retains, trains, develops, and helps you motivate the best so the company can attain and maintain a competitive edge. Think of the coaching staff on a championship sports team.

The professionals in the HR department also keep abreast of ever-changing employment law so they can advise you what to do and not to do while managing your people in order to keep yourself and the company out of court.

RECRUITMENT

INSIDE, OUTSIDE, OR OUTSOURCED?

When you have an opening, you can fill it by hiring from outside or promoting from inside. Considering both sources provides a broader pool of candidates. Furthermore, an outsider can provide a fresh viewpoint, give you the opportunity to increase the diversity of your workforce, or add new skills to the company's capabilities. But the downside is ignorance of your organization that requires time and training to rectify. You also are likely to be more certain of an insider's capabilities. But by far, the most important benefit of promoting from within is the positive message it sends your people: Work hard and you will progress.

If you hire outsiders, pay particular attention to their "fit" with the corporate culture. Skills and knowledge can be taught, but personal chemistry resists change. Many companies use psychological tests to weed out candidates who can't work well in a team environment. Some companies even have members of the team with the opening conduct the candidate interviewing, testing, and hiring.

However, be careful not to unconsciously create a homogenous organization that lacks the diversity of culture, viewpoint, and experience you need to achieve creativity and improve market knowledge and connection. These days, diversity is a recruitment goal of most smart and successful companies.

Proctor & Gamble relies on promoting from within and has a very complete system for tracking high-performance employees and assuring that they get the broad experience necessary to climb the corporate ladder to a leadership position. That's why just retired Chairman A.G. Lafley is confident that the P&G "bench" will deliver fully developed replacements for today's top managers when they retire. [3]

Other options include outsourcing the work or hiring a temporary employee. Both provide more flexibility than hiring a full-time employee. Both also avoid or reduce the overhead cost of benefits, which usually add at least 30 percent to a position's salary. And temporary employees provide a safety valve that can enable a company to lay off workers during a downturn in the economy.

You should routinely consider these options in order to minimize structure. The final option is not filling the position. When an opening occurs, always ask whether the position adds enough value to justify refilling it.

The over-riding consideration in recruitment is excellence. If you hire the very best raw material you can afford, provide proper training and motivation, and have a bit of luck, you'll win more often than you lose.

RETENTION/TRAINING/ DEVELOPMENT

As I noted, Peter Drucker said the best employees are volunteers because they can get a job anywhere. He also pointed out that sustainably successful companies tend to treat employees as an asset, not a cost. What is the link?

If you treat employees (or team members as many companies now call them) as a cost, a safety valve to be used in booms and abused in busts, you are unlikely to create the trust, teamwork, commitment, and excellence that form the foundation of long-term success. Instead, it's likely that you will generate cynicism, mediocrity, and high turnover in your workforce.

What you really want to do is *hire* and *keep* the best. How do successful companies do this?

> First, they offer competitive benefits and wages. You cannot recruit the best unless your basic package is at least equal to the industry average. That's why HR departments closely monitor economic conditions and other companies' actions.
>
> Second, they offer greater rewards (bonuses, stock, etc.) if the company does exceptionally well. They base the rewards on both individual and team value added, not time served. As former GE Chairman Jack Welch puts it, if you don't reward your top performers well, regardless of seniority, you'll lose them. 4 Remember, they're volunteers. Some companies use a double-bonus system to reward both individual and team performance. Incidentally, the benefit of a bonus is that it is one-time; it does not permanently increase the company's labor costs by becoming part of base pay as would a merit raise.
>
> Third, they offer training, development, and opportunity for advancement; and they very systematically develop the next generation of leaders. GE is superb at this. Your best performers often are natural leaders and they eventually want to run something. If you don't give them a chance to do so, some other company will. Note that the traditional route of advancement has been to move up a rung on the orga-

nizational ladder. Today's flatter companies reduce the opportunity for this "climbing-the-ladder" path. Some companies try to solve this problem by separating titles from worth and pay.

Fourth, they offer a feeling of belonging and self-fulfillment through achievement. In short, a satisfying place to work. As Abraham Maslow noted in his hierarchy of needs, this is the primary motivator for high-performing people.

Fifth, they find what employees want and reward them with it. And they evolve the rewards to match the changing desires of succeeding generations.

And finally, they always let you know how you are doing with timely and accurate performance feedback.

PERFORMANCE APPRAISALS

Work with your people to set their individual goals. Monitor performance using key performance indicators (KPIs) such as "sales" or "profits." Measure the gap between goals and results. Mutually devise and institute corrective measures. When the goals are fully achieved, raise them for the next cycle and do it all again. That's the essence of a performance appraisal system that will drive continuous improvement.

If the goals are difficult to quantify—for example "improve employee relations"—you might have to use trait or behavior appraisals. "Does this person exhibit leadership traits and behavior?" But keep in mind that this approach can be viewed as subjective, opening you and the company to a lawsuit if you downgrade or fire the person reviewed.

When conducting a performance review, always start with something positive. "I like what you have accomplished in this area ..." Be as concrete as possible and use tactful, not harsh, language that focuses on improvement, not criticism. Express confidence in the employee's ability to improve and agree on a timetable for improvements to be achieved.

I often asked my direct reports to keep a running record of their accomplishments against goals. I would then invite them to write their own review, which I would go over with them. Of course, I also kept my own records. As Ronald Reagan once said of the Russians, "Trust, but verify." [5]

A considerable body of research asserting that this way of presenting performance reviews doesn't work has accumulated over the past few decades. Researchers say that an individual's need to suppress "cognitive dissonance" (inputs from the environment that disagree with your viewpoint, threatening your self-image) acts like a mental shield that rejects criticism. No matter how constructively and tactfully it is communicated, the individual will not change behavior. This is particularly true if the criticism comes from a superior.

Much of the research demonstrates that *extrinsic* rewards such as merit raises or bonuses are not nearly as effective at motivating desired behavior as is the *intrinsic* reward of self-fulfillment at the top of Abraham Maslow's Hierarchy of Needs.

In his recent book, *Management Rewired,* Charles Jacobson suggests that the solution to this impasse is already evolving. Changing the source of the review from the manager to the individual's teammates appears to get around some of our mental shield. The team members, guided by the manager, select their own goals, decide team and individual rewards, and rate one another's performance. This discovery will continue the evolution of the manager's role from out-in-front, command-and-control alpha figure to a coach using Socratic questioning ("What do you think?") to subtly inspire, guide, and support a team.

NOW WHAT?

You have established an ethical, caring corporate culture committed to excellence. You have created a detailed, far-seeing plan to attack the market. You have built a logical, flat, adaptive structure populated with the best and brightest and empowered them to create value. Now what?

When I went to high school, Latin—one of the long-dead roots of English—was still taught. Consequently, Latin phrases still pop into my mind occasionally. *Scientia est potestas* means knowledge is power. That's the next step, the fuel that will light the engine of the wonderful machine that you and your colleagues have built and send it whirring up the tracks toward success.

You need accurate, timely, reliable, complete, and relevant information to fuel your collective decision-making. And the hardware and software to collect, arrange, and analyze it get better and more affordable every day. Companies that learn to adopt and expertly use information technology (IT) can build competitive advantage.

What is IT? Simply put, it is the hardware, software, and techniques for: 1) acquiring, 2) organizing, 3) storing, 4) manipulating, 5) analyzing, and 6) communicating information. It is the electronic genie released from the bottle. It is the magnifying power that has helped make team structures efficient, global coordination possible and a huge leap in business productivity a reality.

Supply chains, market analysis, R and D, price modeling, trade flows and regulation, and many other business factors all have become global and complex. And they continue to become more so every day. Mountains of data have to be analyzed and turned into *actionable* information to fuel decision-making.

Much of this analysis has become a machine task. But for complex, ambiguous, and uncertain situations, no computer system can yet replace human judgment. Computers are fast and persistent but not intuitive. That's why the best computer still is the one between your ears.

One of the primary benefits of IT is the ability to collapse time as it does in product development. In the auto industry, for example, it used to be that many prototypes of a new model would be physically developed, tested, refined, re-tested, and further refined before a final version would be ready for production. This exacting, "cut-and-fit" process would take thousands of engineers several years and hundreds of millions of dollars to complete. Today, much of the development, refinement, and testing occurs electronically inside computers, shortening the new-vehicle development cycle to as little as twenty months and saving many millions of dollars.

IT also links geographically distant engineering capabilities in a shared database that can be used twenty-four hours a day by various teams scattered all over the earth. Sophisticated IT also enables much better integration of suppliers into the product development process, increasing product quality. And finally, these advances also enable automakers to update models more frequently, better matching the ever-quickening evolution of consumer taste.

As a manager, you need to pay attention to the cost, capability, and compatibility of IT.

Today, IT is an integral part of building competitive advantage, so you can't avoid using it. But it can be hugely expensive. So you need to assure that the investment is justified. Carefully determine your particular needs; assure that the system is customized to fit them; and make sure it can efficiently and effectively communicate with the other systems already in your hands and also, if possible, with those used by key suppliers.

Then implement the new system properly:

- Analyze the situation and assure that the potential system will fully enable you to deal with it.
- Build employee buy-in and support for the new system by soliciting their input during the planning stages.
- Train, train, and train.
- Measure improvement in the KPI's the new system was supposed to affect.
- Adapt/improve and keep moving forward.

As the IT invasion of corporate America grew, it was amazing how many companies bought new capability that could not fully communicate with the expensive "legacy" systems they already had, creating a tower of Babel within the organization. IT advances quickly, so you're always caught between the "rock" of wanting the latest and greatest and the "hard place" of perhaps having to update what you already have in order to assure communication compatibility and cost effectiveness.

Like so much in managing, IT decisions require you to balance several factors. Most large corporations have a Chief Information Officer (CIO) tasked with assuring that cost, effectiveness, and compatibility are assured as new IT systems are put into place to protect the company's information-processing edge or at least maintain competitive parity.

By increasing information accessibility and distributing decision responsibility, IT has changed the way companies are organized. Like a virus, it has invaded corporate neural networks—broadening, flattening, and speeding them up.

Because it provides much more timely and accurate information to your people, some of the decision-making power migrates from you to them. Consequently, you must manage them in a more collaborative fashion while still assuring that you maintain control. Another balancing act.

ORGANIZING TECHNIQUES AND TOOLS

Look in/look out; design your structure to suit your internal resources and the external environment. Then keep it up to date and always as simple, lean, flat, and adaptable as possible. Your primary goal is to improve and accelerate your responsiveness to customers.

Use cross-functional teams to link, coordinate, magnify, and focus "silo" power through diversity, collaboration, and synergy.

Badly designed structure can smother initiative, leadership, and creativity, so make certain any structure you create encourages rather than discourages these important characteristics.

Assure that managers have full control over the functions for which they are responsible and the necessary incentives and KPIs to motivate and measure performance. Don't stretch spans of control too far.

As you decentralize and empower, reinforce the corporate "compass" culture to assure shared vision, focus, and consistency in decision-making. Also clarify responsibility. Without accountability, empowerment is likely to fail, not succeed.

IT can greatly broaden your information horizon and increase productivity. But it has downsides too. For example, computers can seduce people into thinking that sitting in a glass box, sending e-mails is managing. If anything, you need to increase walk-around, face-to-face contact because computers broaden and facilitate access to actionable information, diffusing power and decision-making throughout the organization. It's your job as a manager to make certain that distributed leadership and electronic empowerment actually achieve the company's goals.

Like bread dough, structure wants to rise and expand. Your people always want more people, so they can do more. They also believe that more people will increase their importance in the company. And they will try to reward with promotion, eventually fragmenting management spans and creating too much vertical structure housing more chiefs than braves.

One of the problems with today's flatter, broader structures is that there are fewer levels to provide promotion opportunity. Structure also is expensive, and it usually slows corporate reaction time. To avoid these consequences, force your people to focus on the essential, not the nice to have. Force them to justify any increase in structure by proving that it will return more in customer value than it costs.

Be stingy. Staff for the mean, not the extremes. You might miss some sales during peak demand, but you also may avoid laying hundreds of people off when the business cycle bottoms out.

One of my colleagues recently pointed out to me that there are two primary forms of leading. The first (pushing) works well in a smart company that uses cross-functional teams and continuously evolves and improves through PDCA. The second (pulling) is best suited to a company in crisis that requires quick, revolutionary change to survive. Both styles are well described by Kolp and Rea in their book *Leading With Integrity,* published by Atomic Dog in 2006.

A pushing leader stands behind her people, providing tools, training, resources, coaching, and encouragement. She has a knack for turning abstract strategy into simple, actionable tactics and enough empathy to "read" people skillfully. In order to build their coping skills and assure that they get the credit when goals are achieved, the pushing leader empowers her people to deal with the particular situation and guides their efforts from the rear. She suggests rather than commands. Her favorite phrase is, "What do you think?" She listens carefully to your answer, and she rarely micromanages you.

In contrast, the "pulling" leader works from the front. He is the very visible person on a white horse who lights the burning platform for change and leads the company out of the wilderness. His favorite phrase is, "Follow me!" The most vital skill for this type of leader is authentic, inspirational, emotionally-based communication that connects with and unifies people. A pulling leader builds a bridge from *is* to *can be* and inspires others to cross it with him. No one will follow an unconvincing leader over the bridge. That's why strong, persuasive communication capability is an essential leadership skill.

General Dwight Eisenhower defined leadership in a very pragmatic way: "Convincing the other fellow to do what you want him to when you want him to do it." 1 There are few better examples of this knack than an incident during the Civil War described in the book *Killer Angels* by Michael Shaara. It occurred a few hours before the Battle of Gettysburg.

The central character was Union Army Colonel Joshua Chamberlain, definitely a "pulling" leader. He commanded the Maine 20th Regiment. At this point, he was a young, inexperienced officer who just a year or so before had been a professor at Maine's Bowdoin College. Highly educated, he was fluent in several languages and also a powerful communicator.

Chamberlain was ordered to accept 120 mutineers from the Maine 2nd Regiment who had unknowingly signed three-year contracts when most of the other members of the regiment had signed two-year obligations. When the two-year militia men headed home, the three-year men mutinied because they weren't allowed to leave as well.

Chamberlain's commanding general gave him three choices:

1) Convince them to fight

2) Take them into battle under guard

3) Execute them

Even though he knew it was the riskiest option, Chamberlain chose strategy number one. When the mutineers arrived, he ordered the guards to unshackle them and leave. He called the mutineers "honorable men" who didn't need shackles and guards. Then he called for food and water for them and spent five minutes in his tent, listening to their spokesman, Sergeant Bucklin.

Only then did he stand in front of the mutineers to give the most important and persuasive speech of his young life. This is what he said:

> Bucklin has told me of your problem. I'll look into it as soon as possible. But there's nothing I can do today. We're moving out soon. We'll be marching all day and we may be in a big fight before nightfall. But I'll do what I can when I can.
>
> I've been ordered to take you with me. I've been told that—if you don't come—I can shoot you. Well, you know I won't do that. Not to Maine men. So that's that.
>
> But I've been ordered to take you along and that's what I'll do—under guard if necessary. You can have your rifles back if you want them. The whole Reb army is waiting for us up the road a ways and this is no time for an argument. I tell you this—we sure can use your help. We're down below half strength and we need you.

> I don't want to preach, but if you decide to fight alongside us, there are a few things I want you to know. This regiment was formed last fall back in Maine. There were a thousand of us then. There are not 300 of us now. But what remains is choice.
>
> Some of us volunteered to fight for the Union. Some came because we were bored at home and this looked like it might be fun. Some came because we were ashamed not to. Many came because it was the right thing to do.
>
> Most of us never saw a black man back home, but freedom is not just a word. This is a different kind of army. If you look at history, you'll see men fight for pay, for women, or some other kind of loot. They fight for land, or because the King makes them, or just because they like killing.
>
> But we're here for something new. This hasn't happened much in the history of the world. We're an army going out to set other men free.

Bending down, Chamberlain scratched up a handful of black dirt. Holding it up, he continued.

> This is free ground—all the way from here to the Pacific Ocean. No man has to bow. No man is born to royalty. Here, we judge you by what you do. Not by what your father was. Here you can be something.
>
> This isn't about land—there's always more land. It's about the idea that we all have value. We're worth something more than dirt. I never saw dirt I'd die for. But I'm not asking you to come join us and fight for dirt. What we're all fighting for, in the end, is each other.
>
> If you come with us, I'll be personally grateful. But it's your decision. Now we have to move out.

All but six of the 120 mutineers joined Chamberlain and fought at Gettysburg. His augmented regiment turned the tide of battle at a key point on Little Round Top, where the Confederate Army nearly broke through Union lines.

During his years in the army, Chamberlain was wounded six times, rose to brigadier general, and was awarded the Congressional Medal of Honor for his bravery. After returning to civilian life, he became president of Bowdoin College and later in life was Governor of Maine. But I doubt he ever gave such a brief, powerful and pivotal speech again.

What leadership techniques did Chamberlain use to convince the mutineers to cross the bridge with him?

- He connected with them by calling them "honorable men of Maine" and ordering the guards and shackles away.
- He demonstrated care by quickly supplying food and water.
- He began establishing trust by listening to their grievances, promising support when the battle was over, and taking execution off the table.
- He appealed to their pride and self-respect by saying he needed them.
- And he touched their patriotic emotion by showing them that the reason for fighting was nearly unique in history.

Chamberlain was a charismatic communicator. He knew how to get out of his head and heart and into theirs in order to use their needs to help him achieve his goals.

When you read some of the books dealing with leadership, you find that communication capability is only one among a blizzard of "C" words associated with leadership. Others include character, competence, connection, conviction, consistency, courage, caring, compassion, confidence, and charisma.

Alan Kolp and Peter Rea insist that people will not trust and follow a leader unless they perceive that he exhibits at least two of the "C" words: character grounded in virtue, and competence gained from experience. As they put it, if a leader's character isn't virtuous, he won't do the right thing. If he's not competent, he won't do things right. Doing the right thing the right way at the right time is essential for a leader.

They go on to say that courage also is one of the most important leadership characteristics because a leader lacking it will put his personal interests ahead of the organization and his people. Since your people closely watch everything you do, putting yourself first will undermine your credibility and their trust.

In other words, like nearly everything else in business, leadership is grounded in integrity, honesty and virtue that require you to put the best interests of the organization and your people ahead of your own interests. This is the best way to succeed over the long term. Unfortunately, many CEO's don't do so.

How do you select the best course of action when faced by an ethical problem that presents several different potential solutions? Experts have built many different decision-making models to deal with ethical situations. Here is a summary of the most important.

A FRAMEWORK FOR MORAL DECISION-MAKING

BY MANUEL VALASQEZ, CLAIRE ANDRE, THOMAS SHANKS, MICHAEL J. MEYER

Get the facts and measure them against your values to determine the gap between what *is* and what *should be.* Then use any or all of these five approaches to examine potential solutions and reach a conclusion.

1. Utilitarian Approach:

   Conceived by nineteenth-century philosophers Jeremy Bentham and John Stuart Mill, this approach says the best decision should provide the greatest good for the greatest number.

2. Moral Rights Approach:

   Propounded by eighteenth-century philosopher Immanuel Kant, this approach says people have the right to freely choose what they will do with their lives, the right to be told the truth, the right to do and say whatever they choose in their personal lives so long as it does not violate the rights of others, the right to not be harmed unless they freely choose to risk injury, and the right to expect promises to be fulfilled.

3. Fairness/Justice Approach:

   This approach is based on the teachings of Aristotle, who said, "Equals should be treated equally and unequals unequally." Is your decision even-handed, or does it instead favor some while discriminating against others?

4. Common Good Approach:

   Rooted in the teachings of Plato, this approach requires your decision to benefit the common good we all share (systems, policies, institutions, the law, the environment, etc.).

5. Virtue Approach:

   Also taken from Plato, this approach asks, "Will this decision align with, support, and develop factors all of humanity should strive for?" Factors such as honesty, courage, compassion, generosity, fidelity, integrity, fairness, self-control, and prudence.

Ethical decision-making models can be useful. But when I faced an ethical situation, I usually asked myself three questions that never failed to energize my moral hardwiring:

- Will this course of action help or harm the company's reputation and results?

- Will my decision affect some stakeholders differently than others? If so, have I rank-ordered the stakeholders correctly?
- Would I be embarrassed if I described this decision to my Mom?

I always found the mom test the most useful way to determine whether I was comfortable with a potential decision. Another effective way to test your comfort level is to imagine the decision described on the front page of the local newspaper with your name attached to it.

ETHICS POLICE

Growing public expectations cause government to create new more demanding regulations to prod business behavior in an ethical direction. For this reason, many mid-sized to large corporations have created a high-level position called the ethics officer. Often, the corporate general counsel will carry this additional title and oversee the creation, communication, and enforcement of the firm's ethics and diversity training programs.

NEGOTIATION

Sometimes, despite personal conviction and persuasive communication skills, you will encounter colleagues who want to follow a different path than the one you lay out.

You might have to use two important leadership skills to head off or minimize controversy that could undermine support for the necessary decision.

Negotiation can take two different paths to your desired result. Compromise *shares the pain* because everyone sacrifices something to the other participants. This approach assumes a fixed amount of resources that can be allocated differently but can't be increased.

In contrast, collaboration assumes that resources can be increased or used more efficiently by a new, more productive approach jointly created by the participants during the negotiation. This way of tackling the problem *shares the gain.*

In facilitating negotiation, concentrate on the participants' needs, not their demands. Participants often lay out demands they know are unrealistic simply to see if they can maximize their results. That's why you should concentrate on the needs that are the foundation for successful negotiation. Get all of them out on the table, and then find the common ground upon which all participants can agree. Obviously, collaboration is the most productive approach.

Many companies offer negotiation skills as part of corporate training most employees undergo. The training can underline the need for productive conflict that increases examination of more potential alternatives rather than angry finger-pointing. Other useful techniques for managing conflict include job rotation (walk in the shoes of the person you disagree with) or, if absolutely necessary, transfer of the objector to another division in the company or termination. In any case, the potential benefits of acceptable conflict should be made crystal clear in the corporate culture.

ORGANIZATIONAL POLITICS

You can greatly reduce the likelihood that your decisions will be challenged by making skillful use of organizational politics. As long as they are used to achieve organizational goals that benefit everyone instead of serving self-interest, political skills can be very useful.

Immediately upon joining an organization, you should be looking for future leaders in your "class" with whom you can network and consult as you all rise in the corporation. You can depend upon this group of unpaid consultants for ideas and for support in the negotiations that are an integral part of business. For instance, in Japanese companies, the results of most negotiations are decided outside of meetings and before the final meeting that results in action. Japanese businesspeople call this process *nemawashi,* which means "cultivation of the roots."

RESPONSIBLE FOR REPLICATION

Companies that achieve sustainable success usually have very effective succession planning that delivers the right person at the right time to take over the reins. P&G and GE are superb at developing skillful, well-trained, and experienced leaders at the right time. It's a sure bet that both of these very successful companies are using these difficult times to "stretch" and test future leaders with the difficult assignments a major recession provides.

As a leader, you have a duty to know when it's time for you to leave and who should replace you. This responsibility has a very long tail. You should continually look for leadership qualities, skills, and traits in the people you work with. As you identify these future leaders, you should work to assure that they progress through jobs that will pull them out of their comfort zones and give them the experience necessary to replace you and others in your class at the right time. One of the paramount objectives of this process is to test their worthiness to lead by assigning them tough tasks. As Abraham Lincoln said, "If you want to test a man's character, give him power." [3]

LEADERSHIP LESSONS FROM THE LEDGE

So what tools and techniques should we put in the leading drawer? The selection process begins with a personal story.

In my teens, I was what swimming instructors called "negatively buoyant," a confusing term that meant I sank like a stone unless I moved my hands and feet very enthusiastically. Consequently, I hated the water and didn't learn to swim until forced to by the swimming test required to graduate from my boarding school. When I later joined the US Navy, part of the officer training was an "abandon-ship" drill requiring a jump into deep water from a ledge about twenty feet above it. This frightened me nearly to death. I later experienced some of the same feeling when asked to lead my first business team.

Like leaps of faith into deep water, leading became easier with experience. I observed senior executives; analyzed, adopted, or adapted the best of their styles and techniques; and practiced on my peers until I built a style that was comfortable and effective. Here are the most important leadership lessons I learned.

- As a leader, your primary task is to connect and commit your people to each other and to the best interests of the organization. You can't achieve the authentic communication required to do so without emotion. But depend primarily on facts if you want to persuade people to follow you.
- You're only as good as those around you. Hire people smarter than you and listen to them; they'll make you smart and the company successful.
- Inspire them to aspire by frequently asking, "Why not?" instead of "Why?"
- Don't waste time, effort, and anxiety on things you can't affect.
- Accept a responsibility only if you also receive the authority to fulfill it. This can be difficult to do, particularly in Japanese companies where spans of control sometimes have fuzzy borders that create gray areas.
- Check your title and ego at the meeting-room door. Arrogance is self-defeating; and ambition belongs in the gas tank, not at the steering wheel.
- As you gain position and power, don't allow the trappings of office to isolate you from your people. It will make them reluctant to tell you the truth.

- Don't hide in your office, sending e-mails. Nothing can beat walking around and talking with people face-to-face. Also, establish a channel where confidential sources can be fully candid about what is happening. In many companies, this channel is the chief ethics officer.

- It's best to have people work *with* you, not *for* you. *For* can create envy. *With* usually creates teamwork.

- Take the time to understand. "Let me see if I understand what you just said," is a useful way to successfully close a communication loop.

- Someone once said, "Don't let the apparently urgent tyrannize the genuinely important." Make time for *reflection,* one of the most important leadership skills.

- Because responsibility is part of your job description, failures belong to you. Victories belong to your people. Credit them, not yourself, for success.

- Squeeze all the learning you can out of mistakes, and use it to improve.

- When sacrifices must be made, make certain you sacrifice as much or more than your people.

- Use brutally honest self-examination to find and understand your blind spots. Then try to work around those you can't eliminate. Many companies put their employees through training to hone this skill.

- Coach, don't command. "What do you think?" followed by an intense stare usually yields something much more useful than your own advice.

- Polish your people-picking skills so you can match managers with situations where they have a good chance to succeed.

- People will live *up* or *down* to your expectations. Make goals clear and demanding. Then empower, encourage, and support your people to reach. Help those who can't do so to find a new job at a competitor.

- Walk your talk; every one is watching.

- Don't confuse popularity with respect. The first is nice. The second is vital. And remember that you must give it to get it.

- To gain influence, you must accept responsibility. Jesus put it this way: "Whoever wishes to be the most important and first in rank must be a slave to all." 4

- Start every day by asking, "How can I create value?" Finish every day by asking, "What value did I create?"

- At least once a week, ask yourself and your people: 1) What in our environment has changed? 2) Can it affect our organization? 3) If so, is it a threat or an opportunity? 4) What actions do we need to take?

- Realize that courage is not the absence of fear; it is controlling your fear longer than anyone around you.

- And finally, never confuse your ass with the chair it's sitting in. The job is important; you aren't.

I tried but frequently failed to live up to these demanding rules. Some of them will fit your particular leadership style; some won't. But the most important lesson I learned is that in the final analysis, leadership is a singular pursuit. After listening to everyone's ideas, usually *you* alone must make the final decision. That's why you need to define center and hang onto it.

In *Setting the Table,* Danny Meyer describes a lesson from fellow New York City restaurateur Pat Cetta that shows how important it is for leaders to remain centered.

> Pat pointed to the table next to us. "Take everything off that table except the saltshaker," he said. "Leave it by itself in the middle of the table. Where is the saltshaker now?" he asked.
>
> "Right where you told me to leave it," I replied, "in the center of the table."
>
> "Are you sure that's where you want it?" he asked.
>
> I looked closely. The salt shaker actually was about a quarter of an inch off center. I moved it slightly to what looked like the exact center. Pat then reached out and pushed it three inches off center. "Return it to where you want it," he said.
>
> I re-centered it and he reached out and pushed it six inches off center, saying "Now where do you want it?" Once again, I returned it to center.
>
> "Listen," he said. "Your guests and your staff will always move your salt shaker off center ... That's their job! It's your job to move it back to center. Let them know exactly where you want it. Let them know what excellence looks like to you. And if you're ever willing to let them decide where center is, just give them the keys to the place and quit!"

While he advocates using consistent "gentle pressure," Meyer stresses the absolute need for leaders to define and defend the organization's center (values, vision, mission, and strategy all wrapped up in the company culture). If you do so, people will understand the need for it. If you listen to them, use what they teach you and don't flinch when hard decisions must be made, they will respect you. And if you also consistently follow these leadership practices with as much charm, good nature, and fairness as you can, people will want to do what you want them to when you want them to do it.

Controlling is the most expansive management function. It's everywhere. In fact, I'm not sure it deserves its own drawer because so much of it is buried in the other drawers. For example, it's the "C" (for check) in the PDCA cycle that is the heart of "Planning," it's the function of key performance indicators in the "Organizing" drawer, it's at the heart of the process every time you sit down with one of your people to review her performance, and it's the intention of management by objectives (MBO), a procedure created and popularized by Peter Drucker.

It's hard to pin down because it lurks everywhere. But control's most explicit use probably is to root out and recycle wasted or underutilized resources that can be more productively deployed elsewhere. That's what I'll briefly describe in this section.

There are only three tools in the "Controlling" drawer: a yardstick, a pencil, and a shovel. The yardstick is to measure the distance between performance and goals and drive the PDCA cycle that endlessly tries to close the gap. The pencil is to draw borders for people to stay inside of or to breach with new ideas. And the shovel is for digging *out* root causes and digging *up* treasure. In other words, solving problems and recycling waste into value.

Finding the root cause of a problem is like removing a stubborn weed with a long tap root. If you don't dig down and get all of it, the weed will simply grow back. At Toyota, the heart of the digging process is called "the five whys." When you think you have totally uncovered the root cause, ask yourself why you think so. When you have carefully and completely answered yourself, you are likely to discover that you need to dig some more. Keep repeating this procedure until you are certain that you have dug all the way down to the tip of the root. Unless circumstances force a premature decision, you should devise and implement a solution to the problem only when you have the entire root in your hand.

You also need to dig for the waste in everything you do, extract value from it that you can use elsewhere, and apply controls to assure that it doesn't crop up again. It's this function that I want to focus on. Let me start with a personal example.

My wife and I like wine, so I built a modest wine cellar into our retirement home. Since I can access a much broader selection of intense and interesting wines directly from small vintners by ordering over the Internet, UPS, and FedEx often deliver cases of wine to our door. This has made me aware of freight costs.

Recently, we enjoyed a bottle of one of the few premium wines I possess. The bottle felt massive in my hand. Curious, I put it on the kitchen scale and determined that it weighed 73 ounces (more than four and a-half pounds). After dinner, I weighed it again and determined that the empty bottle weighed 44 ounces. Then I weighed the box the twelve bottles came in and found another 40 ounces.

If I have done my math correctly (not always a sure thing with me), the twelve-bottle case contained approximately thirty-three pounds of glass, two and a half pounds of cardboard and Styrofoam, and twenty-two pounds of wine. Even though they contain and protect the wine, from a customer viewpoint, the glass, cardboard, and Styrofoam are waste. FedEx charged about $22 to ship the glass, $10 to ship the wine, and $4 to ship the box from Paso Robles, California to Rock Hill, South Carolina.

As they realize the wastefulness of shipping lots of heavy glass simply to make a marketing statement ("It's heavy, so it must be good."), some winemakers are beginning to explore alternatives. For example, one maker of French Beaujolais has begun to use light-weight plastic bottles for its product. *Business Week* calls it "Beaujolais Plastique." [1] I expect continually rising transportation costs to make value chain believers of many more wineries in the future.

A value chain is simply the collection of activities that provides products or services to customers. It includes (among other activities): market research, product design and development, component and part production, manufacturing and assembly, sales, service and recycling—in short, virtually every activity included in a modern company. That's one reason why the control function is buried all over the toolbox.

If every step of the long process from materials to market is not continuously examined and controlled to minimize input while maximizing output, waste will occur. Earlier, I described an optimized "just-in-time" (JIT) value chain where the sourcing of parts from suppliers that begins production is activated only by the "pull" of true customer demand at the other end of the chain.

In the "Organizing" section, I warned of the temptation to activate idle production capacity in reaction to the "push" of expensive structure and the pressure it creates to book a profit. This can stack up unsold inventory (both parts and finished products) in the value chain. In other words, it sucks in and transforms capital, labor, and material into idle, sit-around waste, not customer-pleasing value.

Remember, productivity is achieved by minimizing the value of input and maximizing the value of output. Reducing supplies of parts and finished goods at your facility is a mirage if you don't police the entire value chain. Even if you don't see them, parts stored at your suppliers or finished goods stored at your distributor are waste buried in the price they will charge you. Waste devours profit wherever it exists along the path from supplier to customer.

But reducing waste by reengineering a sloppy process or implementing just-in-time (JIT) parts delivery is only one of the benefits provided by a lean system. Switching to JIT from JIC (just in case) also can reveal other problems lurking within your production process.

Think of it as lowering the level of a river to reveal the rocks disrupting smooth flow so you can dig them out. When a worker can no longer reach for a stored-on-the-premises JIC part to cover a process flaw, the kinks and glitches that devour energy and slow the river down become visible. This enables you to find and attack the root cause rather than slapping a band-aid on a symptom. It also will improve product quality because avoiding or recycling waste and creating quality are two sides of the same coin.

Time and human energy are expensive resources that can easily be wasted by inattentive management. Reworking defective products eats up both. Product planning and development also can gobble up an inordinate amount of time and energy, putting you behind faster competitors that will seize the first-mover advantage you wanted to grab. That's why good managers use concurrent (all design phases working simultaneously), not consecutive ("I'm done with my portion, now you can begin yours.") engineering to collapse time, reducing man hours and cost.

Excessive energy usage also can drive costs up. Despite short-term ups and downs, over the long term, the cost of conventional energy will inexorably rise because it is created from ultimately limited resources much in demand by rapidly growing economies such as China and India. The cap-and-trade measures currently being hammered out by Congress to address global warming also will drive business to reduce energy usage. Shipping costs will have to be continually reduced. This will require shortening supply lines by, for example, co-locating key suppliers (particularly of bulky or heavy components) around final assembly operations instead of continuing to rely on a geographically dispersed supply chain. This strategy will be further accelerated by companies' efforts to reduce their carbon footprint because obtaining parts from distant sources generates rail and road emissions that have a negative environmental impact.

In addition, if you don't closely and continuously monitor your entire supply chain, you put your organization's reputation at risk. A *Business Week* article titled "Made in China, Sued Here" [2] described the increasing number of lawsuits being filed against US corporations with tainted overseas supply chains.

Lawyers have gone after companies such as Del Monte, which sold pet treats made with tainted Chinese ingredients. William Ruskin, an attorney for a law firm suing Del Monte, pointed out the need for companies to keep contaminated or defective material out of their supply chains. "All you have to show is that the product was defective. It's no defense to say we didn't know."

A Wall Street Journal article by Emily Parker, an assistant editorial features editor, highlights the anything-for-profit attitude behind China's contamination crises.[3]

"Some Chinese will protest that the current wave of panic—which came to a head with restrictions by America's FDA on several kinds of Chinese seafood—is overblown, and the majority of Chinese goods are perfectly safe. But others don't want to live in an environment where brushing your teeth can be a death-defying act."

Ms. Parker sums up the situation this way. "The larger problem is that in a country without a real rule of law, where everything is subject to Communist party interpretation, there is no codified set of ethics to guide national behavior."

Another WSJ article by Jeremy Haft highlights how difficult it is to assert control in an era of global sourcing. "On average, it takes China seventeen separate parties to produce a product that would take us three. China's industries are composed of hundreds of thousands of tiny factories and firms—plus traders, brokers, haulers, and agents, all of whom take control of the goods and materials but add little value to the product. With every additional player in the chain, cost, risk, and time grow. In this environment, effective quality control is difficult." [4]

The Chinese government reacts in an unusual but very direct way to companies that create dangerous or toxic products. They execute the company's CEO. Although the US government doesn't yet shoot guilty CEO's, the message for American companies is clear. If you source globally to control cost, you must police your entire supply chain or your company's reputation may be tarnished and you may be jailed.

SHAREHOLDERS STAKEHOLDERS AND EXECUTIVE COMPENSATION

As business has become more global, complex, and competitive, demand and compensation for top executives have grown—particularly in the United States. According to a *Wall Street Journal* survey [1], in 2008, the CEO's of 200 large American companies earned an average of about $7.6 million (including long-term incentives). This is anywhere from one hundred to three hundred times the pay of the average American worker, depending upon which source you select and whether or not benefits and long-term compensation are included. Some sources say the ratio is even higher.

By contrast, the Hay Group says the median pay for European CEOs is about 40 percent of the US median. The average annual compensation for the CEO of a large Japanese company rarely exceeds $1 million—no more than twenty to twenty-five times the pay of the average Japanese manufacturing employee and little different from the salaries of other top executives at the company. Most Japanese CEOs grow up in their company, finally making it to the top after a thirty-to-forty-year climb. And many of the executives they grew up with are on the company board with them. Towers Perrin consultant Naohiko Abe says the typical Japanese CEO thinks, "These are my long-time colleagues. It is hard to provide higher compensation to myself."[2] This attitude and these compensation practices may be one reason why Japanese companies are more risk-averse and teamwork-oriented than most American corporations.

This is a complex and difficult issue. Because it's a convenient and accepted way to measure growth in a company's value, most of the hurdles American CEOs must leap to justify their lofty pay are tied to increasing shareholder return (stock price, stock splits, dividends, etc.). Their rewards for doing so usually are stock grants or options with a long-term vesting feature designed to foster a long-term outlook. Instead, it too often causes them to focus on what is personally rewarding rather than fair and effective. The news media usually focus on the eye-popping size of the total award and fail to explain to their readers, listeners, and viewers the long-term vesting and other requirements. Consequently, the general public has no idea of the complexity of the award or what targets must be met to gain it. They focus solely on its size and get angry.

Fortune columnist Geoff Colvin (Fortune January 18, 2010, P. 22) describes a new measure called EVA (economic value added) momentum created by consultant Bennett Stewart. Colvin describes it as, "profit after deducting an appropriate charge for all the capital in the business." He notes that using it as a yardstick creates long-term value. He also notes that Gilead Sciences, Google, and Apple—with EVA momentum of 24.3 percent, 22.7 percent, and 12.1 percent respectively—are the current EVA leaders among US companies.

EVA might just be a more effective target than focusing primarily on shareholder satisfaction, which I believe can incentivize a short-term viewpoint that adversely impacts the interests of other stakeholders. I also believe that treating stakeholders more equally and always putting the key stakeholder, the customer, first can create the desired long-term viewpoint.

Think of a company as a stool supported by three legs—money, material, and manpower—with the length of each leg denoting the value management places on it. If money is valued over the other two legs, the stool gets out of balance and unstable. For example, if the relative importance placed on high-quality parts shrinks, management might degrade supplier margins to protect company profits and shareholder return. Or if, in order to keep shareholders happy, management values current return over long-term growth, the R&D budget may be squeezed, undercutting efforts to maintain future competitive advantage. If management considers employees a cost rather than an asset, the CEO is likely to fire or retire many of them in order to reduce cost, increase productivity, preserve shareholder return, and—not so incidentally—justify his or her high pay. You get the behavior you reward. If maximizing shareholder return is the target, top management will likely focus solely on it instead of ethical and practical actions that benefit the company's health and competitiveness over the long term.

Such short-term thinking can seduce executives into regarding a company only as a balance sheet designed to reward them and shareholders, not as a place that also provides employment, generates commitment, and creates value for customers and communities as well as investors. This tendency can be magnified in cyclical industries where structure added to exploit booms is routinely cut during busts.

Schumpeter might applaud this "creative destruction" from his grave, but it deeply angers the American public. According to a *Business Week* survey [3], in calendar year 2000, CEOs of firms that laid off a thousand or more workers (cutting cost and increasing productivity) earned about 80 percent more than the average CEO of the 365 companies in the survey—$24 million in total compensation versus $13 million for the average CEO included in the survey. Mark Hurd, CEO of Hewlett-Packard is an example. Last year, Hurd earned total compensation of $42.5 million. In May, he laid off about six thousand employees and cut the salaries of the survivors by 5 to 15 percent. [4] Many Americans interpret this approach as "the more people you put into the unemployment line, the more you earn." What a perverse incentive.

There is a saying in the auto industry: "You can't cut your way to prosperity." Always valuing shareholders over employees, distributors, and suppliers will not create the loyalty, commitment, and teamwork necessary to satisfy the most important stakeholders: customers. Only excellent products created by committed, creative employees will. If you lay them off, you may not have the expertise to successfully participate in the economic recovery.

I can't overemphasize the need to define success in a carefully balanced way. It is the foundation upon which you build the strategy you then motivate your people to achieve. You get the results you reward, so make very certain you are aiming at the right targets.

Unfortunately, there is a harsh reality called the business cycle. How do the best companies deal with large economic fluctuations? What safety valves do they use? How do they try to cut costs humanely?

When addressing labor costs, many companies reduce work hours or pay. Some deal with rising market demand by hiring "temporary" or contract employees paid a lower wage and denied benefits. They make it clear to these employees that if demand remains good, some of them might eventually be hired on as full-time employees. But they also make it clear that they will be the first to go when tough times require cost-cutting.

According to *BusinesssWeek* magazine (1–18–10), the current recession has created so many permanent "temporary" employees that a recent Conference Board survey found that only 45 percent of workers are satisfied with their job, the worst result in the survey's twenty-two-year history. Discouragement of this level can devastate a company's performance and it has virtually wiped out the job-for-life culture my generation was accustomed to.

Excessively compensating CEO's who fire employees they (or their predecessors) hired to chase now-vanished opportunities also creates public resentment. According to a recent study by the Institute for Policy Studies, 77 percent of Americans believe CEOs earn too much. The 2008–09 financial meltdown and infusion of taxpayer money into business has provided government the perfect excuse to pander to this populist resentment by curtailing executive pay. And indeed, as I write, the Obama administration is considering ways to do so and even shareholders are fighting to have "*a say on pay.*"

This won't be the first time government has capped top-management pay. In the midst of the Great Depression, President Roosevelt and Congress capped executive pay. The American public was outraged that Bethlehem Steel President Eugene Grace made $1.62 million in 1929 ($20.5 million in today's dollars). [5]

During my years in Washington, I met many ethical, effective, and admirable people who became politicians because they believed in honest public service. I also met many arrogant, self-centered ones who have forgotten (if they ever knew) that they derive their authority "from the consent of the governed," in other words, from us. In the Declaration of Independence, America's founding fathers explicitly and eloquently stated the right to revolt against the misuse of centralized government power. They later enshrined it in the Constitution and the Bill of Rights. "To secure these rights, governments are instituted among men, deriving their just powers from the consent of the governed: that, whenever any form of government becomes destructive of these ends, it is the right of the people to alter or abolish it and to institute new government."

You won't succeed in business if you forget who employs you. Unfortunately, in government amnesia occurs frequently.

It also has been my experience that once you let a politician or regulator into your business, it is very difficult to get him out. Many of them want to replace the "invisible hand" of the marketplace with the "visible hand" of government regulation. Citing "fairness" as their goal, they want to create equal *outcomes* for everyone, not just the equal *opportunity* promised by the US Constitution and the Bill of Rights. To reach this goal, they strive to create a nanny state where rewards are not earned but instead are granted by a ruling elite in return for support. Many also have viewpoints that rarely focus beyond the next election. Unfortunately, the longer they stay in government, the stronger these viewpoints tend to become. This creates the "ass-and-chair confusion" described in the leadership chapter.

Why is this so dangerous? George Washington said, "Like fire, government is a dangerous servant and a fearful master." When Congress passes a law, the special interest groups (including companies) that gave it life strive to keep it alive so the benefits they receive will continue as long as possible. While a company must evolve its business plan to stay in step with a continuously changing marketplace, government answers to no such competitive imperative. That's why most politicians are unlikely to change or kill a law that pleases their supporters and assures a free flow of campaign funding, even if the original *need* for it has disappeared. Ronald Reagan described government programs as the nearest thing to eternal life on the planet.

What's the lesson for business? Beware of powerful people with short-term viewpoints and long-term impact. For example, one likely result of pay caps is that the most able executives will abandon the partially nationalized "companies in crisis" where they are most needed for more successful companies that refused government subsidies and the accompanying pay limits. This persuasive evidence of the power of supply and demand is a perfect example of the unintended consequences government frequently creates.

Creating genuine value with conservative and collaborative management practices clearly could have avoided much of the current economic and political mess. Instead, the situation is generating financial turmoil, personal pain, huge government debt, regulatory overreach, and the long-term involvement of powerful people with little understanding of or respect for the free-market foundation and emphasis on individual freedom and responsibility that make the United States nearly unique among the nations of the world.

Some of them actually express contempt for the market-driven economy that has made the US so amazingly successful for generations. They also consider the Constitution and the Bill of Rights "living" documents that need to evolve. In their urgent haste to "fix" everything and their unwarranted certainty that they can do so, they are likely to pile on enough unintended consequences to transform the United States from leader to laggard.

Business invited this result by violating commitments inherent in its implied contract with society. Top executives and the directors to whom they supposedly answer should have been wiser. Instead, they opened the door to politically-driven intervention.

THE IMPLIED SOCIAL CONTRACT

Peter Drucker eloquently described a viewpoint that could have avoided this mess:

> There are management tools and techniques, concepts and principles, and perhaps even a universal discipline called management... But management also is a culture and a system of values and beliefs... through which a society makes productive its own values and beliefs... to serve the common purposes of mankind.[6]

WE MAKE THINGS

This insight from Drucker matches a more cryptic comment from someone I worked with. I had just finished a presentation to the Toyota Motor Corporation board. As usual, Dr. Shoichiro Toyoda—a member of Toyota's founding family—sat near the center of the row of Japanese gentlemen across the long table as I and one of my outside lobbyists described the schemes and strategies of various groups in Washington DC that wished Toyota less success than we envisioned.

As the board members milled about after the presentation, Dr. Toyoda approached. A short, upright man with thick, salt-and-pepper hair and intelligent eyes, he is an engineer by training and a hands-on executive who enjoys touring Toyota plants around the world to see the Toyota production system in action.

I was still going on to someone about political dangers when the doctor looked at me and said, "Olson-san, never forget that we make things." We make things—a short sentence concealing a world of meaning. Here's how I understood his comment.

Toyota and many other honest, well-managed companies make:

- high-quality products and services to satisfy demanding customers
- exciting jobs where people can find fulfillment
- community contributions in the form of taxes, payroll, philanthropy, and expertise
- profit that funds social as well as material progress and enables the company to continue making all of the above

I believe Dr. Toyoda was implying that as long as Toyota makes things society values, the company also will be valued and allowed to succeed. In the long run, *public and customer support created by ethics, excellence, and value is any company's best defense.*

WE PACKAGE DEALS

Now imagine a similar conversation with one of the architects of the current credit mess. In an unusual burst of candor, he looks over your head (never into your eyes) and says in a lofty voice, "I and my colleagues package complex deals you can't be expected to understand." Let me also translate: "We package deals."

Egged on by community organizers, entitlement addicts, and vote-hungry politicians, these clever, greedy people:

- Enticed millions of trusting people into debt they didn't understand and couldn't afford
- Packaged the debt in complex financial instruments (collateralized debt obligations) like a dishonest grocer hiding bad peaches by putting good ones on top
- Persuaded rating agencies to endorse their peaches
- Sold them to financial institutions around the world too ignorant, too trusting, too lazy, or too greedy to fully understand or care what they were buying who then convinced insurers to protect them against the possibility of default with credit default swaps (CDS) that evade some key regulations governing insurance companies
- This entire chain of clever people then said, "Not our fault," when the gigantic river of toxic debt they unleashed undermined and collapsed the foundation of the global financial system that provides capital without which many well-managed companies can no longer employ people to "make things."

The most vital point is left unsaid. This "spread-the-risk" packaging (called "securitization" by financial wizards who use it) so dilutes the provider-consumer relationship that ethical responsibility, customer focus, brand strength and transparency—the bedrock fundamentals of conservative business practices—evaporate. Some would say that this creativity was unleashed by the free-market forces I applaud. But the key missing ingredient is *ethical integrity.*

In the November 16, 2009, edition of *Business Week,* Blackstone Group co-founder Peter G. Peterson described the results of these attitudes this way:

> American business has been on the defensive for a decade—tarred by scandals at Enron and WorldCom, excoriated for excessive executive pay, and, most recently, scarred by the perception that government has rescued many financial institutions whose greed and shortsightedness led to the worst economic crisis since the Great Depression. It shouldn't surprise us that opinion polls show that Americans and their leaders in Washington hold U.S. business in low esteem.

WHAT ARE THE KEY LESSONS?

Prompted by these examples, what key management lessons should you take away with you?

- Management is the science and art of pursuing excellence and delighting customers in order to create corporate profit and long-term value. In the US, crucial byproducts of this pursuit are national economic progress and a lifestyle envied by other countries.

- Business transforms four inputs (money, manpower, material, and information) into one output: customer-defined value. If this is done efficiently, effectively, consistently, and creatively, customers will buy your output, funding you to continue delighting them. Government cannot create wealth; only business can. Government can only *confiscate* wealth (by taxing) or *borrow* it (by taking on debt future generations of taxpayers will have to repay).

- The basic tools and techniques to achieve business goals are conservative, ethical and practical. They change very slowly, if at all.
- At sustainably successful companies, the tools are embedded in an urgent, competitive "learning" culture that is constant at its core; adaptive at its margin; and based on skeptical, fact-based decision-making.
- These companies never waste a crisis. Instead, they recognize it as an opportunity to improve every aspect of their operations.
- They also know that success can make you complacent. That's why they spend more time analyzing and solving problems than celebrating victories.
- They treat all stakeholders as business partners who deserve honest respect and a fair share of the value they help create.
- They try to be very clear about company goals and relentless in pursuit of them.
- Nurturing and strengthening this sort of corporate culture requires smart, authentic, emotionally connected leaders who seek, learn and teach, balancing principle with pragmatism and discipline with creativity.
- These leaders extract extraordinary performance from ordinary people by empowering, encouraging, supporting, rewarding, coaching, and holding them accountable.
- They and the successful companies they work for maintain a margin of safety; they continuously exam-

ine the world and evolve their plans and processes to stay in step with the changing environment; they question assumptions and rarely overreach.

- They know that pride can create competitive spirit, but hubris lives next-door. That's why they never take positive coverage of their company too seriously.
- They relentlessly control cost, drive out waste, enforce ethical behavior, minimize structure, and produce abundant results from scarce resources.
- If they have to destroy formerly successful but now ineffective strategy and structure, they try to minimize the adverse impact of this "creative destruction" on their workforce and apply the "freed-up" resources to new approaches more likely to succeed.
- They conserve resources during good times in order to—among other things—build competitive advantage in bad times.
- They do everything they can to assure the success and survival of the organization because without it there is no value-creation.
- When sacrifice is necessary, these leaders make certain it is shared fairly by all stakeholders—beginning with themselves. Mutual success and sacrifice create *trust,* the mortar that holds these principles, practices, tools, and techniques together.

WITHOUT TRUST, THERE IS NO BOTTOM LINE

Although relatively easy to understand, management is difficult and demanding to do. And it includes dealing with many ongoing problems that have no ideal solution.

At the heart of business is a transaction process that creates expectations. If I loan you money, I believe you will pay me back. In fact, the word *creditor* is based on the Latin word *credo,* which means "I believe." If you don't pay me back, I won't loan to you again. If you buy a product from me, you expect it to fulfill my promises. If it doesn't, you won't buy from me again.

Without trust, this transparent transaction process cannot occur. Businesses that remember this and follow simple, conservative, trust-building practices generally succeed. Those that allow stupidity, cupidity, or arrogance to lure them off-course generally fail.

I'm certain some clever and successful business people would call my emphasis on core values, conservative practices, and ethical behavior naïve and unrealistic. Obviously, I disagree. But let me call on a much better-known business commentator to answer these critics. Jim Collins wrote the best-selling business books *Built to Last* and *Good to Great.* He is now working on a book that examines how successful companies navigate through turbulent times.

In a recent interview, Collins had this to say about the importance of core values:

> In times of great duress, tumult and uncertainty, you have to have moorings. Companies like P&G, GE, J&J, and IBM have an incredible fabric of values, underlying ideals or principles that explain why it is important that they exist... The more challenged you are, the more you have to have your values. You need to preserve them consistently over time. [1]

All I can add is *amen.*

> Every morning in Africa, a gazelle awakes knowing it must outrun the quickest lion or die. Every morning, a lion awakes knowing it must outrun the slowest gazelle or starve. Whether you are a gazelle or a lion, every morning hit the ground running. [2]

FOREWORD

1. *Brainyquote.com*
2. *Business Week* 6/9/08
3. *The Essential Wooden* by John Wooden and Steve Jamison

PLANNING

1. *The Yale Book of Quotations* edited by Frank Shapiro
2. Wikipedia
3. Wikipedia
4. *Contemporary Management* by Jones and George (chapter 8)
5. Wikipedia
6. Wikipedia
7. Brainyquote.com
8. Brainyquote.com
9. Dow Jones Industrial website
10. *Fortune* 5/5/08
11. Wikipedia

12. Personal experience
13. *The Three Musketeers* by Alexandre Dumas
14. *Fortune* 7/21/08
15. *Business Week* 7/20/09
16. *Economist* 6/25/09
17. *Wall Street Journal* 7/12/09
18. *The Yale Book of Quotations*
19. Brainyquote.com
20. Wikipedia
21. *The Yale Book of Quotations*
22. A Brief Historical Tour
23. 1–14 Wikipedia

ORGANIZING

1. *Setting the Table*
2. Wikipedia
3. *Fortune* 4/13/09
4. *Business Week* 2/5/09
5. *The Yale Book of Quotations*

LEADING

1. *Ike: An American Hero* by Michael Korda
2. *The Yale Book of Quotations*
3. *The Yale Book of Quotations*
4. *The Bible* (Mark 9:35)

CONTROLLING

1. *Business Week* 9/29/08
2. *Business Week* 4/10/09
3. *Wall Street Journal* 8/10/07
4. *Wall Street Journal* 7/8/07
5. *Business Week* 6/8/09

SHAREHOLDERS, STAKEHOLDERS, AND EXECUTIVE COMPENSATION

1. *Wall Street Journal* 4/3/09
2. *USA Today* 11/10/09
3. *Business Week* 3/10/09
4. *Business Week* 5/25/09
5. *Fortune* 11/23/09
6. Wikipedia

CONCLUSION

1. *Fortune* 2/2/09
2. *The Earth Is Flat* by Tom Friedman

Contemporary Management (fifth edition) by Gareth R. Jones and Jennifer M. George

Management Rewired by Charles S. Jacobs

How Markets Fail by John Cassidy

Moral Intelligence by Doug Lennick and Fred Kiel

The Essential Wooden by John Wooden and Steve Jamison

Ike: an American Hero by Michael Korda

Setting the Table by Danny Meyer

Killer Angels by Michael Shaara

Joshua Chamberlain: the Soldier and the Man by Edward G. Longacre

The Earth is Flat by Tom Friedman